VALID 2019

The Eleventh International Conference on Advances in System Testing and Validation Lifecycle

November 24 - 28, 2019

Valencia, Spain

VALID 2019 Editors

Jos van Rooyen, Identify - Software Quality Services, the Netherlands

Samuele Buro, University of Verona, Italy

Marco Campion, University of Verona, Italy

Michele Pasqua, University of Verona, Italy

Printed from e-media with permission by:

Curran Associates, Inc.
57 Morehouse Lane
Red Hook, NY 12571

Some format issues inherent in the e-media version may also appear in this print version.

Printed with permission by Curran Associates, Inc. (2020)

International Academy, Research, and Industry Association (IARIA)
412 Derby Way
Wilmington, DE 19810

Phone: (408) 893-6407
Fax: (408) 527-6351

petre@iaria.org

Additional copies of this publication are available from:

Curran Associates, Inc.
57 Morehouse Lane
Red Hook, NY 12571 USA
Phone: 845-758-0400
Fax: 845-758-2633
Email: curran@proceedings.com
Web: www.proceedings.com

Table of Contents

VALID 2019

Forward

The Eleventh International Conference on Advances in System Testing and Validation Lifecycle (VALID 2019), held on November 24 - 28, 2019- Valencia, Spain, continued a series of events focusing on designing robust components and systems with testability for various features of behavior and interconnection.

Complex distributed systems with heterogeneous interconnections operating at different speeds and based on various nano- and micro-technologies raise serious problems of testing, diagnosing, and debugging. Despite current solutions, virtualization and abstraction for large scale systems provide less visibility for vulnerability discovery and resolution, and make testing tedious, sometimes unsuccessful, if not properly thought from the design phase.

The conference on advances in system testing and validation considered the concepts, methodologies, and solutions dealing with designing robust and available systems. Its target covered aspects related to debugging and defects, vulnerability discovery, diagnosis, and testing.

The conference provided a forum where researchers were able to present recent research results and new research problems and directions related to them. The conference sought contributions presenting novel result and future research in all aspects of robust design methodologies, vulnerability discovery and resolution, diagnosis, debugging, and testing.

We welcomed technical papers presenting research and practical results, position papers addressing the pros and cons of specific proposals, such as those being discussed in the standard forums or in industry consortiums, survey papers addressing the key problems and solutions on any of the above topics, short papers on work in progress, and panel proposals.

We take here the opportunity to warmly thank all the members of the VALID 2019 technical program committee as well as the numerous reviewers. The creation of such a broad and high quality conference program would not have been possible without their involvement. We also kindly thank all the authors that dedicated much of their time and efforts to contribute to VALID 2019. We truly believe that thanks to all these efforts, the final conference program consists of top quality contributions.

This event could also not have been a reality without the support of many individuals, organizations and sponsors. We also gratefully thank the members of the VALID 2019 organizing committee for their help in handling the logistics and for their work that is making this professional meeting a success. We gratefully appreciate to the technical program committee co-chairs that contributed to identify the appropriate groups to submit contributions.

We hope the VALID 2019 was a successful international forum for the exchange of ideas and results between academia and industry and to promote further progress in system testing and validation. We also hope Valencia provided a pleasant environment during the conference and everyone saved some time for exploring this beautiful city.

VALID 2019 Steering Committee

Andrea Baruzzo, IDS Interaction Design Solutions, Italy
Tadashi Dohi, Hiroshima University, Japan

VALID 2019 Industry/Research Advisory Committee

VALID Publicity Chair

VALID 2019

Committee

VALID Steering Committee

Andrea Baruzzo, IDS Interaction Design Solutions, Italy
Tadashi Dohi, Hiroshima University, Japan
Roy Oberhauser, Aalen University, Germany
Patrick Girard, LIRMM / CNRS, France
Stefan Wagner, University of Stuttgart, Germany
Hiroyuki Sato, University of Tokyo, Japan
Mehdi Tahoori, Karlsruhe Institute of Technology (KIT), Germany
Hironori Washizaki, Waseda University, Japan

VALID Industry/Research Advisory Committee

Xinli Gu, Huawei, USA
Sigrid Eldh, Ericsson AB, Sweden
Jos van Rooyen, Identify - Software Quality Services, the Netherlands
Miroslav N. Velev, Aries Design Automation, USA
Philipp Helle, Airbus Group Innovations, Germany

VALID Publicity Chair

Ayman Aljarbouh, University of Grenoble Alpes (UGA) in Grenoble, France
Lorena Parra, Universitat Politecnica de Valencia, Spain

VALID 2019 Technical Program Committee

Wasif Afzal, Mälardalen University, Sweden
Jitendra Aggarwal, Arm, India
Ayman Aljarbouh, University of Grenoble Alpes (UGA) in Grenoble, France
Amir Alimohammad, San Diego State University, USA
María Alpuente, Technical University of Valencia (UPV), Spain
Moussa Amrani, Namur Digital Institute, Belgium
Aitor Arrieta, University of Mondragon, Spain
Sebastien Bardin, CEA LIST | Paris Saclay, France
Kamel Barkaoui, Conservatoire National des Arts et Metiers, France
Cesare Bartolini, ISTI - CNR, Pisa, Italy
Andrea Baruzzo, IDS Interaction Design Solutions, Italy
Saddek Bensalem, Université Grenoble Alpes/Verimag, France
Ateet Bhalla, Independent Consultant, India
Bruno Blaskovic, University of Zagreb, Croatia
Sergiy Bogomolov, Australian National University, Australia
Mohamed Boussaa, University of Rennes 1 | INRIA, France
Laura Brandán Briones, Universidad Nacional de Córdoba, Argentina
Mark Burgin, University of California Los Angeles (UCLA), USA

Samuele Buro, University of Verona, Italy
Vinicius Cardoso Garcia, Universidade Federal de Pernambuco, Brazil
Laura Carnevali, University of Florence, Italy
Adnan Causevic, Mälardalen University, Sweden
Federico Ciccozzi, Mälardalen University, Sweden
Bruce Cockburn, University of Alberta, Canada
Hichem Debbi, University of Mohamed Boudiaf-M'sila, Algeria
Gulsen Demiroz, Sabanci University, Istanbul, Turkey
Stefano Di Carlo, Politecnico di Torino, Italy
Dario Di Nucci, Vrije Universiteit Brussel, Belgium
Daniel Dietsch, University of Freiburg, Germany
Luigi Dilillo, LIRMM (Laboratoire de Informatique Robotique et Microélectronique de Montpellier), France
Tadashi Dohi, Hiroshima University, Japan
Dimitris Dranidis, CITY College | International Faculty of the University of Sheffield, Greece
Rolf Drechsler, University of Bremen/DFKI, Germany
Lydie du Bousquet, Université Grenoble-Alpes (UGA), France
Sigrid Eldh, Ericsson AB, Sweden
Marie Farrell, University of Liverpool, UK
Hermann Felbinger, Graz University of Technology / AVL List GmbH, Austria
Jicheng Fu, University of Central Oklahoma, USA
Gregory Gay, University of South Carolina, USA
Patrick Girard, LIRMM / CNRS, France
Xinli Gu, Huawei, USA
Bidyut Gupta, Southern Illinois University, Carbondale, USA
Kazumi Hatayama, Gunma University, Japan
Philipp Helle, Airbus Group Innovations, Germany
Lom Messan Hillah, Université Paris Nanterre / Sorbonne Université / CNRS - Laboratoire d'Informatique de Paris 6 - LIP6, France
Zoltán Horváth, Eötvös Loránd University, Budapest, Hungary
Hassan Ibrahim, Université Paris Sud, Université Paris Saclay, France
Daisuke Ishii, University of Fukui, Japan
Bo Jiang, Beihang University, Beijing, China
David Kaeli, Northeastern University, Boston , USA
Ahmed Kamel, Offutt School of Business | Concordia College, USA
Marouane Kessentini, University of Michigan - Dearborn, USA
Narges Khakpour, Linnaeus University, Sweden
Takashi Kitamura, National Institute of Advanced Industrial Science and Technology (AIST), Japan
Moez Krichen, Al-Baha University, Saudi Arabia / University of Sfax, Tunisia
Herbert Kuchen, University of Münster, Germany
Maurizio Leotta, University of Genova, Italy
Bruno Lima, University of Porto / INESC TEC, Portugal
Chu-Ti Lin, National Chiayi University, Taiwan
Francesca Lonetti, ISTI-CNR, Italy
Lei Ma, Harbin Institute of Technology, China
Libero Maesano, Simple Engineering, France
Hans Manhaeve, Ridgetop Europe nv. / Ridgetop Group inc., Belgium
Eda Marchetti, CNR-ISTI, Pisa, Italy

Abel Marrero, Bombardier Transportation Signal Germany GmbH, Germany
Mieke Massink, CNR-ISTI, Pisa, Italy
Rivalino Matias Jr., Federal University of Uberlandia, Brazil
Amin Milani Fard, Simon Fraser University, Vancouver, Canada
Andreas Morgenstern, Fraunhofer Institute for Software Engineering (IESE), Germany
Roy Oberhauser, Aalen University, Germany
Pablo Oliveira Antonino, Fraunhofer IESE, Germany
Yassine Ouhammou, LIAS/ISAE-ENSMA, France
Lorena Parra, Universitat Politecnica de Valencia, Spain
Giovanni Pau, Sorbonne Universitè, Paris, France
Adriano Peron, University of Naples "Federico II", Italy
Roberto Pietrantuono, Università di Napoli Federico II, Italy
Pasqualina Potena, RISE SICS Västerås, Sweden
Paolo Prinetto, Politecnico di Torino, Italy
Claudia Raibulet, University of Milano-Bicocca, Italy
Oliviero Riganelli, University of Milano Bicocca, Italy
Mehrdad Saadatmand, RISE SICS Västerås, Sweden
Giedre Sabaliauskaite, iTrust Centre for Research in Cyber Security | Singapore University of Technology and Design, Singapore
Hiroyuki Sato, University of Tokyo, Japan
Josep Silva Galiana, Technical University of Valencia, Spain
Marjan Sirjani, Mälardalen University, Sweden / Reykjavik University, Iceland
Maria Spichkova, RMIT University, Australia
Andrea Stocco, University of British Columbia - Vancouver, Canada
Mehdi Tahoori, Karlsruhe Institute of Technology (KIT), Germany
Salvador Tamarit, Universitat Politècnica de València, Spain
Bedir Tekinerdogan, Wageningen University, The Netherlands
Spyros Tragoudas, Southern Illinois University, USA
Jos van Rooyen, Identify - Software Quality Services, the Netherlands
Miroslav N. Velev, Aries Design Automation, USA
Enrico Vicario, University of Florence, Italy
Arnaud Virazel, Université de Montpellier / LIRMM, France
Stefan Wagner, University of Stuttgart, Germany
Hironori Washizaki, Waseda University / National Institute of Informatics / SYSTEM INFORMATION, Japan
John Wiegley, BAE Systems, UK
Kristian Wiklund, Ericsson AB, Sweden
Robert Wille, Johannes Kepler University Linz, Austria
Cemal Yilmaz, Sabanci University, Istanbul, Turkey
Haibo Yu, Shanghai Jiao Tong University, China
Pavol Zavarsky, Concordia University of Edmonton, Alberta, Canada

Copyright Information

Towards an Operational Semantics for Solidity

Marco Crosara
Dept. of Computer Science
University of Verona, Italy
Email: marco.crosara@studenti.univr.it

Gabriele Centurino
Dept. of Computer Science
University of Verona, Italy
Email: gabriele.centurino@studenti.univr.it

Vincenzo Arceri
Dept. of Computer Science
University of Verona, Italy
Email: vincenzo.arceri@univr.it

Abstract—**Solidity is a multi-paradigm programming language used for writing smart contracts on the Ethereum blockchain and offers a wide range of features, such as Ethereum transfers between contracts or wallets of normal users. Its specification is not formally defined, the behaviours of Solidity constructs are informally provided by its documentation, leading to misunderstandings and buggy code. Without a formal semantics, reasoning about programs becomes extremely hard, if not impossible. In this paper, we provide a first-step towards a formal operational semantics for Solidity, defining a memory model for the language, able to capture its main features.**

Keywords–Programming Languages; Solidity; Semantics.

I. Introduction

We intend to define a complete semantics of a core of Solidity [1], but this is not a simple task. In order to reach this goal, we have to deal with an unusual actor: the blockchain [2]. Due to its presence, providing a formal semantics for Solidity [3] could result challenging for two reasons. The first one is relative to the frequently updating language, since Solidity continuously changes the constructs and mechanics of operations [4]. For this reason, in this work, we have chosen a specific version of the compiler: 0.5.10. The second one is that we have to deal with the Storage of the blockchain, that is separated from the memory of the Ethereum Virtual Machine (EVM). In this paper, we provide a first step toward a formal semantics of Solidity, modelling the memory and the interaction that happens between a smart contract and the blockchain. In the next section, we describe the Solidity language, the domains and the memory model used. In Section III we present its concrete semantics for some basic constructs and in Section IV we extend the semantics to contracts and functions. Finally, we provide some ideas for future related works.

II. Solidity

Solidity is the most popular language to write smart contracts on the Ethereum blockchain. Intuitively, a smart contract is a computer program designed to execute some actions when some condition is verified [2]. Solidity has been designed to offer a simple way to develop a smart contract and for this reason, it is strongly inspired by JavaScript. Unlike JavaScript, it is object-oriented and statically typed. When we deploy a contract on the blockchain, the Solidity code has to be executed by the EVM. Inside this environment, we have a set of instructions called opcodes that are encoded in byte code in order to have a more efficient store. Each opcode has a cost of execution, this is needed to prevent the execution of infinite loops or similar and to reward the miners who validate the transactions. This cost is expressed in unit of Gas and the price per unit is expressed in GWei, a fraction of an Ethereum token. 1 Ethereum (ETH) corresponds to 1×10^{18} Wei, that are 1×10^{9} GWei. For the sake of simplicity, we assume that any operation inside the blockchain has been equipped with enough gas to correctly end its execution. In our work, we chose not to handle transactions in memory, studying only the interaction that they have with the blockchain.

A. Memory and Storage

Solidity provides three types of memory, namely Stack, used to hold local variables of primitive type (*uint256*, *bool*, etc.), Storage is a persistent memory and is a key-value store where keys and values are both 32 bytes, storing, for instance, state variables. Finally, Memory is a byte-array that contains data until the execution of the function, used to save, for example, function arguments. In this paper, we do not distinguish between Stack and Memory. According to the real model described, the evaluation of expressions and statements in our work is made considering the tuple $\sigma = \langle N_\rho, \rho, C, A \rangle$. We can split this tuple in two halves, namely Memory and Storage. The first one refers to the EVM Memory and the second one to the blockchain. N_ρ e ρ are respectively the Namespace and the link between address and values. Instead A stands for Accounts and contains the balances of contract address and normal user address. C stands for Contracts and contains, for any contract, the corresponding Storage and all the functions with the corresponding signature. Formally, we define the State σ, as follows.

- $N_\rho \in$ Memory is a function s.t. $N_\rho : \textsc{Id} \rightarrow \textsc{MLoc}$

```
contract Bank {
  uint money = 0;
  constructor () public payable {
    money = msg.value;
  }
  function sendEther () public payable {
    money += msg.value;
    if(money > 300000000000000000){//0.3 ETH
      msg.sender.transfer(money);
      money = 0;
    }
  }
  function () external payable {}
}
```

Figure 1. Example of a simple contract written in Solidity.

Solidity ::= (Contract)*
Contract ::= `contract` *id* { (St)* }
St ::= Method | StateDef
StateDef ::= Type *id* ;
| Type *id* = Exp ;
Type ::= `uint` | `bool` | `address` | `address payable`
Method ::= `function` *id*((Type *id*,)*) (Qualifier)* {(Stmt)*}
| `function()external payable` { (Stmt)* }
| `constructor`((Type *id*,)*) `public` | `internal` { (Stmt)* }
Qualifier ::= `public` | `internal` | `external`
| `private` | `returns`(Type *id*)
BinOp ::= + | - | * | / | % | && | || | == | !=
| > | < | >= | <=
UnOp ::= - | !

Stmt ::= ϵ
| Type *id* (= Exp)? ;
| `if`(Exp) Stmt (`else` Stmt)?
| `while`(Exp) Stmt
| { (Stmt)* }
| `return` (Exp)? ;
| Exp ;
Exp ::= Literal
| *id*((Exp ,)*)
| *id*`.transfer`(Exp)
| Exp BinOp Exp
| UnOp Exp
| *id* = Exp
| *id*
Literal ::= $n \in$ UINT | $b \in$ BOOL | $a \in$ ADDR | $\widetilde{a} \in$ ADDR_{P}

Figure 2. Syntax of Solidity core.

- $\rho \in$ Memory is a function s.t. ρ : MLOC $\to$ V with V = UINT $\cup$ BOOL $\cup$ ADDR $\cup$ ADDR_{P}
- $A \in$ Storage is a function s.t. A : ADDR $\to$ UINT
- $C \in$ Storage is a function s.t. C : ADDR $\to \langle \lambda, N_\mu, \mu \rangle$ Where $\lambda = \langle P, I, E, R \rangle$, N_μ : ID $\to$ SLOC and μ : SLOC $\to$ V

λ contains contracts functions that are divided by access level: Public, Internal, External, PRivate $\langle P, I, E, R \rangle$, each element in λ is also a function $\langle$ID, ForParams$\rangle \to$ BODY and ForParams is a list of $\langle$Type, ID$\rangle$ but for simplicity, sometimes we will refer to it with a string of the type (Type *id*,)*. BODY is a string with a sequence of statements: (Stmt)*. The qualifier of a function can be [4]:

- `public`: Public functions are part of the contract interface and can be either called internally or via messages.
- `internal`: Those functions and state variables can only be accessed internally (i.e., from within the current contract or contracts deriving from it), without using this.
- `external`: External functions are part of the contract interface, which means they can be called from other contracts and via transactions. An external function f cannot be called internally.
- `private`: Private functions and state variables are only visible for the contract they are defined in and not in derived contracts.

In this paper, we suppose that in each moment we have another namespace N_σ, which determines the last declaration of a variable, between Memory and Storage. Formally, it is always $N_\sigma = (\sigma.C(\dot{c}).N_\mu)[N_\rho]$ where $\dot{c}$ is the current contract address.

B. Domains

The followings are the Solidity domains considered for this paper:

- $n \in$ UINT = { 0, 1, 2, ..., $2^{256} - 1$}: the domain of Unsigned Integers, corresponding to the *uint256* type in the Solidity language. We define two numbers, $\tilde{N} = 2^{256}$ and $\hat{N} = 2^{256} - 1$, where $\hat{N}$ is the max value that can be assigned.
- $a \in$ ADDR is the domain of Addresses. The addresses are used as unique identifier inside the blockchain: every contract, every user and every transaction has one. In Solidity the *address* type holds a 20 byte value (size of an Ethereum address), e.g., '0xbb9bc244d798123fde783fcc1c72d3bb8c189413'. The same address could be also declared as Address Payable, this is necessary to allow transfers of ETH on it, as we will explain later. The domain of payable address is ADDR_{P} and with $\widetilde{a}$ we denote an element of it.
- $b \in$ BOOL = {`true`, `false`}: the domain of Booleans.
- $x \in$ ID is the domain of Identifiers. In Solidity, an identifier is a string with the pattern [a-zA-Z_$][a-zA-Z_$0-9]*. An ID element could be a variable name, a contract name or a function name.
- LOC: the domain of Locations. We can have two types of locations, namely Memory Locations (MLOC) and Storage Locations (SLOC). Hence we have LOC = MLOC $\cup$ SLOC s.t. MLOC $\cap$ SLOC = $\varnothing$.

In our work, we denote by type$(\sigma, x) \in$ {`uint`, `bool`, `address`, `address payable`} the type x in σ, e.g., type$(\langle\{x \to l\}, \{l \to 5\}, C, A\rangle, x) =$ `uint`. We abuse notation denoting type(σ, l), $l \in$ LOC, the type of a location.

Address and Address Payable: In our core, there are two ways to declare addresses and the difference is the keyword `payable`. A payable address can be the receiver of some ETH sent using a `transfer` or a `send` function in a smart contract. Trying transfer money to a non-payable address would result in a compiler error. Therefore, for example the `transfer` function could not be invoked on a non-payable address. In sight of this, we can state that the keyword payable is only used in order to force the developer to wisely choose which address should be able to receive ether or not. In our semantics, the meta-variables of address can be interchangeable with the one of address payable.

$$(\!| n |\!)\sigma \stackrel{\text{def}}{=} n,\ n \in \textsc{UInt}$$
$$(\!| b |\!)\sigma \stackrel{\text{def}}{=} b,\ b \in \textsc{Bool}$$
$$(\!| a |\!)\sigma \stackrel{\text{def}}{=} a,\ a \in \textsc{Addr}$$
$$(\!| \tilde{a} |\!)\sigma \stackrel{\text{def}}{=} \tilde{a},\ \tilde{a} \in \textsc{Addr}_{\textsc{p}}$$

$$(\!| e_1 + e_2 |\!)\sigma \stackrel{\text{def}}{=} (n_1 +_{Num} n_2)\%\tilde{N}$$
$$(\!| e_1 - e_2 |\!)\sigma \stackrel{\text{def}}{=} (n_1 -_{Num} n_2)\%\tilde{N}$$
$$(\!| e_1 * e_2 |\!)\sigma \stackrel{\text{def}}{=} (n_1 \cdot_{Num} n_2)\%\tilde{N}$$
$$(\!| e_1 \,/\, e_2 |\!)\sigma \stackrel{\text{def}}{=} (n_1 \,/_{Num}\, n_2)\%\tilde{N} \text{ with } n_2 \neq 0$$
$$(\!| e_1 \,\%\, e_2 |\!)\sigma \stackrel{\text{def}}{=} (n_1 \,\%\, n_2)\%\tilde{N}$$
$$(\!| -e_1 |\!)\sigma \stackrel{\text{def}}{=} (\!| 0 - e_1 |\!)\sigma$$
$$(\!| e_1 |\!)\sigma \stackrel{\text{def}}{=} n_1,\ (\!| e_2 |\!)\sigma \stackrel{\text{def}}{=} n_2$$

```
function checkPlusMin() public
    ↪ returns (uint n5, uint n6, uint
    ↪ n7) {
  uint n1 = 2**256 - 1;
  uint n2 = 1;
  uint n3 = 2**255 + 333333;
  uint n4 = 2**255 + 4444444;
  return (n1 + n2, n3 + n4, 0 - n2);
}
```

```
> checkPlusMin()≫(0,4777777,2**256-1)
```

Figure 3. (a) Identity (b) Arithmetic expressions (c) Example of overflow.

C. Environment access and Memory updating

In our semantics, when we need to access a tuple, for the sake of readability, we use the dots notation. For example, if $\sigma = \langle N_\rho, \rho, C, A\rangle$ we write $\sigma.C$ to access C of σ. Note that, in some cases we will refer directly to $N_\rho, \rho, C, A, \lambda, N_\mu, \mu$ respectively instead of each ones with σ prefixed: $\sigma.N_\rho, \sigma.\rho, \sigma.C$...

Updating of a single value in Memory:

$$\begin{gathered} \rho \in \text{Memory},\ l \in \textsc{MLoc}, \\ k \in \text{V} = \textsc{UInt} \cup \textsc{Bool} \cup \textsc{Addr} \cup \textsc{Addr}_{\textsc{p}} \\ \rho[l \leftarrow k] = \rho' \in \text{Memory} \\ \Longleftrightarrow \\ \rho'(l) = k \text{ and } \forall l' \in \textsc{MLoc}\,.\, l' \neq l\,.\, \rho'(l') = \rho(l') \end{gathered}$$

Updating of a Memory with another Memory:

$$\begin{gathered} \rho, \rho' \in \text{Memory},\ l \in \textsc{MLoc},\ k \in \text{V} \\ Loc(\rho) = \{l \mid (l \mapsto k) \in \rho\} \\ \rho[\rho'] = \rho'' \in \text{Memory} \\ \Longleftrightarrow \\ \forall l \in Loc(\rho) \cup Loc(\rho')\,.\, \rho''(l) = \begin{cases} \rho'(l) & l \in Loc(\rho') \\ \rho(l) & \text{otherwise} \end{cases} \end{gathered}$$

Similarly, we can define Memory namespace update with single value ($N_\rho[x \leftarrow l]$) and update between Memory namespaces ($N_\rho[N'_\rho]$). The same is also true for N_μ, μ, C, A update.

III. Concrete Semantics of Solidity

In this section, we define our core (Figure 2) and we provide a formal semantics for it [5]. We focus the attention on the standard constructs of programming languages, the more blockchain related constructs will be treated in Section IV. There will be also some examples that we will use to motivate the results. The semantics is captured by the function $(\!| \cdot |\!)$ that we will define in the next sections.

A. Expressions Semantics

We denote the domain of expressions by $e \in$ Exp. In this section, we define the main semantics expressions of our Solidity core. The semantics of expressions is captured by the function $(\!| \cdot |\!)$: Exp $\times$ State $\rightarrow$ V $\times$ State, that evaluates an expression in a State and returns a final value, with the previous State modified by the evaluation. For convenience when the State σ does not change the evaluation, it returns only V. As we have already mentioned before, in our core we consider four primitive types: *bool*, *address* (payable and not), and *uint*. Each type has been defined as a domain of its values: UINT, BOOL, ADDR and $\textsc{Addr}_{\textsc{p}}$. According to this, we have four identity rules (Figure 3a). We also have other rules that refer to unary and binary operators. In Solidity, like in every other programming languages, we have many of them but we selected only the ones that have been defined in the syntax. Any numeric operator (Figure 3b) has a correspondent in the concrete. The rules consider the numeric overflow, indeed in UINT we can represent, like previously stated, the max value $\hat{N}$ and we will have an overflow using the next integer ($\tilde{N}$), this one is used by the rules through the modulo operator. A Solidity UINT overflow example is shown in Figure 3c.

The rules regarding *And*, *Or* and *Negation* for the binary operators (Figure 4a) are trivial. It is interesting to talk about *Equality* and *Inequality* operators among the different types. In these rules, we have the operator $\Box \in \{==, !=\}$ and the operator $\boxdot$ that is the numeric counterpart of the first one. For example, if $==$ is the syntactic notation, $=_{Num}$ is the corresponding numeric operator. Each rule checks that the type of e_1 is the same of e_2 and returns a boolean value. An exception is the type $\textsc{Addr}_{\textsc{p}}$ that is equal to ADDR for the reason previously specified. The next rule is similar to

$$(\!| e_1 \,\&\&\, e_2 |\!)\sigma \stackrel{\text{def}}{=} \begin{cases} \texttt{false} & (\!| e_1 |\!)\sigma \stackrel{\text{def}}{=} \texttt{false} \\ (\!| e_2 |\!)\sigma & (\!| e_1 |\!)\sigma \stackrel{\text{def}}{=} \texttt{true} \end{cases}$$

$$(\!| e_1 \,||\, e_2 |\!)\sigma \stackrel{\text{def}}{=} \begin{cases} \texttt{true} & (\!| e_1 |\!)\sigma \stackrel{\text{def}}{=} \texttt{true} \\ (\!| e_2 |\!)\sigma & (\!| e_1 |\!)\sigma \stackrel{\text{def}}{=} \texttt{false} \end{cases}$$

$$(\!| !e |\!)\sigma \stackrel{\text{def}}{=} \begin{cases} \texttt{true} & (\!| e |\!)\sigma \stackrel{\text{def}}{=} \texttt{false} \\ \texttt{false} & (\!| e |\!)\sigma \stackrel{\text{def}}{=} \texttt{true} \end{cases}$$

$$(\!| e_1 \Box e_2 |\!)\sigma \stackrel{\text{def}}{=} \begin{cases} n_1 \boxdot_{Num} n_2 & (\!| e_1 |\!)\sigma \stackrel{\text{def}}{=} n_1 \wedge (\!| e_2 |\!)\sigma \stackrel{\text{def}}{=} n_2 \\ b_1 \boxdot_{Bool} b_2 & (\!| e_1 |\!)\sigma \stackrel{\text{def}}{=} b_1 \wedge (\!| e_2 |\!)\sigma \stackrel{\text{def}}{=} b_2 \\ a_1 \boxdot_{Adr} a_2 & (\!| e_1 |\!)\sigma \stackrel{\text{def}}{=} a_1 \wedge (\!| e_2 |\!)\sigma \stackrel{\text{def}}{=} a_2 \\ \tilde{a}_1 \boxdot_{Adr} \tilde{a}_2 & (\!| e_1 |\!)\sigma \stackrel{\text{def}}{=} \tilde{a}_1 \wedge (\!| e_2 |\!)\sigma \stackrel{\text{def}}{=} \tilde{a}_2 \\ a_1 \boxdot_{Adr} \tilde{a}_2 & (\!| e_1 |\!)\sigma \stackrel{\text{def}}{=} a_1 \wedge (\!| e_2 |\!)\sigma \stackrel{\text{def}}{=} \tilde{a}_2 \end{cases}$$

$$(\!| e_1 \diamondsuit e_2 |\!)\sigma \stackrel{\text{def}}{=} (n_1 \ \diamondsuit_{Num}\ n_2) \in \{\texttt{true}, \texttt{false}\}$$

Figure 4. (a) Boolean expression semantics (b) Relational expression semantics.

the previous, but the operator $\Diamond \in \{>,<,>=,<=\}$ with the counterpart $\Diamond$ is only defined for numerical expressions. Afterwards, we will define other two rules regarding the semantics expressions.

1) Assignment: In this rule and the following ones, we suppose that $\dot{c}$ is the current contract address and that $\sigma = \langle N_\rho, \rho, C, A\rangle$.

$$(\!|\, x = e \,|\!)\sigma \stackrel{\text{def}}{=} \begin{cases} \langle g, \sigma' \rangle \text{ with } g \stackrel{\text{def}}{=} (\!|\, e \,|\!)\sigma & N_\sigma(x) \in \text{MLoc} \\ \langle g, \sigma'' \rangle \text{ with } g \stackrel{\text{def}}{=} (\!|\, e \,|\!)\sigma & N_\sigma(x) \in \text{SLoc} \end{cases}$$
$$\sigma' = \langle N_\rho, \rho[N_\rho(x) \leftarrow g], C, A\rangle$$
$$\sigma'' = \langle N_\rho, \rho, C[\dot{c} \leftarrow \langle \lambda, N_\mu, \mu'' \rangle], A\rangle$$
$$\text{with } \mu'' = \mu[N_\mu(x) \leftarrow g]$$
$$\text{if } N_\sigma(x) \neq \bot$$

The assignment in Solidity depends on the variable x which we are referring to. If $N_\sigma(x) \in$ MLoc it means that the variable has been defined into the EVM Memory (potentially could exist an x inside the Store). In this case, priority is given to the local variable and we only modified ρ based on the address contained in N_ρ. Otherwise, if $N_\sigma(x) \in$ SLoc it means that it does not exist a local variable with that identifier. However, for the precondition rule $N_\sigma(x) \neq \bot$, there is always a global variable x, thus we modify μ associating the evaluation result of e to the Storage address of x.

2) Lookup:

$$(\!|\, x \,|\!)\sigma \stackrel{\text{def}}{=} \begin{cases} \rho(N_\rho(x)) & N_\sigma(x) \in \text{MLoc} \\ C(\dot{c}).\mu(C(\dot{c}).N_\mu(x)) & N_\sigma(x) \in \text{SLoc} \end{cases}$$
$$\text{if } N_\sigma(x) \neq \bot$$

Like the previous rule, when in the code a variable x is used, the returned value is determined with reference to the location where the last declaration happened. According to this, the value of x in the Memory ρ or in the Storage μ is returned.

B. Statements Semantics

In this section, we define the formal semantics of Statements. Let denote by $s \in$ Stmt the sets of statements. With a slight abuse of notation, we denote the statement semantics evaluation with $(\!|\cdot|\!)$: Stmt × State → State, that evaluates a statement in a State σ and returns the State modified by the evaluation.

1) Skip:

$$(\!|\, \epsilon \,|\!)\sigma \stackrel{\text{def}}{=} \sigma \quad \text{where } \epsilon \text{ is the empty statement}$$

2) Lacal Variable Declaration:

$$(\!|\, \texttt{uint } x = e_1;\, |\!)\sigma \stackrel{\text{def}}{=} \langle N_\rho[x \leftarrow l], \rho[l \leftarrow (\!|\, e_1 \,|\!)\sigma], C, A\rangle$$
$$\text{with } (\!|\, e_1 \,|\!)\sigma \in \text{UInt}$$
$$l \in \text{MLoc fresh and } N_\rho(x) = \bot$$

The first semantics rule in this section is the empty statement, the following are regarding the variables declaration. The declaration of local and state variables is syntactically the same, so the correct rule is chosen accordingly to the position of statement. We distinguish if the declaration is inside the body of a function or directly inside the contract. The declaration of a local variable, differently from the only assignment, also modifies N_ρ. Therefore, a new location is added and the evaluated expression will be saved on it.

3) State Variable Declaration:

$$(\!|\, \texttt{uint } x = e_1;\, |\!)\sigma \stackrel{\text{def}}{=} \sigma' = \langle N_\rho, \rho, C', A\rangle$$
$$\text{with } C' = (C[\dot{c}.N_\mu(x) \leftarrow l])[\dot{c}.\mu(l) \leftarrow (\!|\, e_1 \,|\!)\sigma]$$
$$\text{with } (\!|\, e_1 \,|\!)\sigma \in \text{UInt},\ l \in \text{SLoc fresh}$$
$$\text{if } N_\mu(x) = \bot$$

The declaration of state variable is similar but in this case N_μ and μ are modified. In each case, there is a precondition: a variable with the same name must not be already declared. The rules for the other primitives types, which differ from *uint* are easily deducible for similarity.

4) Declaration without initialisation:

$$(\!|\, \texttt{uint } x;\, |\!)\sigma \stackrel{\text{def}}{=} (\!|\, \texttt{uint } x = 0;\, |\!)\sigma$$
$$(\!|\, \texttt{bool } y;\, |\!)\sigma \stackrel{\text{def}}{=} (\!|\, \texttt{bool } y = \mathit{false};\, |\!)\sigma$$
$$(\!|\, \texttt{address } z;\, |\!)\sigma \stackrel{\text{def}}{=} (\!|\, \texttt{address } z = \text{0x0}^{40};\, |\!)\sigma$$

Rules used for the declaration without initialisation can be defined as rewriting of the same rules with assignment. The value assigned to the variable is the default value of each primitive types. Other semantics rules related to constructs in our core in Figure 5a, are the one for `if` (rewrite of `if else`) and for `while`, where the single iteration is based on the rewrite of `if else`. Then, we have the semantics of block: after evaluating the statement inside the braces, the Memory of such evaluation is returned, preserving however the initial namespace N_ρ. This happens because the declaration made inside a block must not be considered as valid outside of it. Examples are presented in Figure 5b and Figure 5c. Finally, for the sequence of statements let's proceed evaluating the first statement. On the state returned we evaluate the next statement.

IV. Concrete Semantics of Contracts

In this section, we provide the operational semantics for contracts and functions. A Solidity file has *sol* extension, it could contain some contracts, which are denoted by c. A file can be considered as a sequence of contracts C. We denote by st a structure type and by St a sequence of structure type. A st could be a state variable or a function. In addition ω is used to denote the constructor of the contract.

1) First:

$$(\!|\, c_1\texttt{C} \,|\!)\sigma \stackrel{\text{def}}{=} (\!|\, \texttt{C} \,|\!)\sigma'' \text{ with } \sigma'' = \langle N_\rho, \rho, C', A'\rangle$$
$$\text{and } \sigma' = (\!|\, c_1 \,|\!)\sigma \stackrel{\text{def}}{=} \langle N'_\rho, \rho', C', A'\rangle$$
$$\text{with } N_\rho, \rho \text{ empty}$$

To evaluate a Solidity file we have to execute the sequence of contracts which it contains. We evaluate every contract on the state returned from the execution of the previous one, replacing however N'_ρ and ρ' with a new empty Memory N_ρ, ρ. Indeed the Memory of the EVM is not preserved from the execution of a contract to an another. Let's make a consideration now: $C(\dot{c}).\lambda.P$ and $C(\dot{c}).\lambda.E$ are visible to all other contracts, but to call a method of another contract it is necessary to create an instance of it, e.g., `MyContract mc = new MyContract();` and that does not

$$(\!| \texttt{if}(e)\ s\ \texttt{else}\ s'\ |\!)\sigma \stackrel{\text{def}}{=} \begin{cases} (\!| s |\!)\sigma & (\!| e |\!)\sigma \stackrel{\text{def}}{=} \texttt{true} \\ (\!| s' |\!)\sigma & (\!| e |\!)\sigma \stackrel{\text{def}}{=} \texttt{false} \end{cases}$$

$$(\!| \texttt{if}(e)\ s\ |\!)\sigma \stackrel{\text{def}}{=} (\!| \texttt{if}(e)\ s\ \texttt{else}\ \epsilon |\!)\sigma$$

$$(\!| \texttt{while}(e)\ s\ |\!)\sigma \stackrel{\text{def}}{=} (\!| \texttt{if}(e)\{s\ \texttt{while}(e)\ s\}\ \texttt{else}\ \epsilon |\!)\sigma$$

$$(\!| \{s\} |\!)\sigma \stackrel{\text{def}}{=} \langle N_\rho, \rho', C', A'\rangle \text{ with } (\!| s |\!)\sigma \stackrel{\text{def}}{=} \langle N'_\rho, \rho', C', A'\rangle$$

$$(\!| s\ s' |\!)\sigma \stackrel{\text{def}}{=} (\!| s' |\!)((\!| s |\!)\sigma)$$

```
function checkBlock()
  ↪ public returns (
  ↪ uint vx, uint vy) {
  uint x = 0;
  uint y = 0;
  { uint z = 0;
    x = x + 1;
    { uint w = 0;
      y = y + 1;
    }
  }
  return (x, y);
}
```

> checkBlock()≫(1, 1)

```
function checkBlock2()
  ↪ public {
  uint x = 0;
  uint y = 0;
  { uint z = 0;
    { uint w = 0; }
    w = w + 1; // <<
  }
}
```

> *Compile error: Undeclared id.*

Figure 5. (a) IfElse, If, While, Block and Sequence of Stmt (b) Example of block: scoping of variables (c) Example of block: undeclared identifier.

exist in our core. Furthermore $C(\dot{c}).\lambda.I$ is directly visible to the contracts that derive from it, but to allow inheritance in Solidity we need the `is` construct that is not inside our core.

2) Contract:

$$(\!| \texttt{contract}\ \mathit{cname}\ \{St\} |\!)\sigma \stackrel{\text{def}}{=} \begin{cases} \sigma'' & \omega \in St \\ (\!| c' |\!)\sigma & \omega \notin St \end{cases}$$

$$c' = \texttt{contract}\ \mathit{cname}\ \{\texttt{constructor()}\ \texttt{public\{\}}\ St\}$$

$$\sigma'' \stackrel{\text{def}}{=} \begin{cases} (\!| C'.\lambda.P(\mathit{constructor}, *) |\!)\sigma' & C'.\lambda.P(\mathit{con...}, *) \neq \bot \\ (\!| C'.\lambda.I(\mathit{constructor}, *) |\!)\sigma' & C'.\lambda.I(\mathit{con...}, *) \neq \bot \end{cases}$$

$$\text{with } \sigma' = (\!| St |\!)\sigma \stackrel{\text{def}}{=} \langle N_\rho, \rho, C', A'\rangle$$

The evaluation of a contract if there is not any constructor, add, firstly, the default constructor. Afterwards, all the structure types contained are evaluated. After that, $C(\dot{c})$ is populated with functions and state variables of the contract. The final step is to execute the constructor code and return the evaluation of it.

3) Function Declaration: For simplicity, we suppose that functions with a return statement at the end of body, have the respective `returns`(Exp) qualifier in the function definition.

$$(\!| \texttt{function}\ \mathit{fname}\ (FP)\ \texttt{public}\ \{\text{BODY}\} |\!)\sigma \stackrel{\text{def}}{=} \sigma'$$

$$(\!| \texttt{function}\ \mathit{fname}\ (FP)\ \texttt{public returns}\ (rp)\ \{\text{BODY}\} |\!)\sigma \stackrel{\text{def}}{=} \sigma'$$

$$\sigma' = \langle N_\rho, \rho, C', A\rangle \text{ with } C' = C[\dot{c}.\lambda.P.\langle \mathit{fname}, FP\rangle \leftarrow \text{BODY}]$$

$$\text{if}$$

$$C(\dot{c}).\lambda.P(\langle \mathit{fname}, FP\rangle) = \bot, C(\dot{c}).\lambda.I(\langle \mathit{fname}, FP\rangle) = \bot,$$
$$C(\dot{c}).\lambda.E(\langle \mathit{fname}, FP\rangle) = \bot, C(\dot{c}).\lambda.R(\langle \mathit{fname}, FP\rangle) = \bot$$

The evaluation of a function declaration is the addition of the same to $C(\dot{c}).\lambda$. For internal and private qualifiers the rule is equivalent, with the modification of I, E and R respectively instead of P.

4) Constructor Declaration: A constructor is optional. Only one constructor for each contract can be defined, which means that overloading is not supported. In the code, no function with name '*constructor*' can be defined. Constructor functions can be either public or internal. If there is no constructor, the contract will assume the default empty constructor.

$$(\!| \texttt{constructor}\ (FP)\ \texttt{public}\ \{\text{BODY}\} |\!)\sigma \stackrel{\text{def}}{=}$$
$$(\!| \texttt{function}\ \mathit{constructor}\ (FP)\ \texttt{public}\ \{\text{BODY}\} |\!)\sigma$$
$$\text{with } \sigma.C(\dot{c}).\lambda.P(\mathit{constructor}, *) = \bot$$
$$\text{and } \sigma.C(\dot{c}).\lambda.I(\mathit{constructor}, *) = \bot$$

The constructor evaluation can be treated as a rewrite of a normal function declaration, with identifier the word '*constructor*'. We use this trick because the Solidity syntax does not allow naming a function '*constructor*'. The rule is the same for `internal` qualifier.

5) Fallback Function Declaration: A fallback function is a particular function that can be inside a contract. It has two mandatory characteristics: it has to be anonymous and does not have any arguments. It is executed whenever a function identifier does not match the available functions or if the contract receives plain Ether without any other data associated with the transaction. For this reason, it is good practice to make it payable, so that it can receive ETH sent erroneously. Consequently, in our core, we choose that the fallback function is always payable. The fallback function has only 2300 units of gas, leaving not much capacity to perform operations except basic logging.

$$(\!| \texttt{function}\ ()\ \texttt{external payable}\ \{\text{BODY}\} |\!)\sigma \stackrel{\text{def}}{=}$$
$$(\!| \texttt{function}\ \epsilon\ (\varnothing)\ \texttt{external}\ \{\text{BODY}\} |\!)\sigma$$
$$\text{with } \sigma.C(\dot{c}).\lambda.E(\epsilon, \varnothing) = \bot$$

The idea of the fallback function semantics is the same as the constructor one. The rule is given as rewrite of function declaration with ϵ, namely the empty string, as name.

6) Return:

$$(\!| \texttt{return;} |\!)\sigma \stackrel{\text{def}}{=} \sigma' = \langle N_\rho[\mathit{return} \leftarrow l], \rho[l \leftarrow \epsilon], C, A\rangle$$
$$(\!| \texttt{return}\ e; |\!)\sigma \stackrel{\text{def}}{=} \sigma' = \langle N_\rho[\mathit{return} \leftarrow l], \rho[l \leftarrow (\!| e |\!)\sigma], C, A\rangle$$

The return statement is the last Stmt of function. It returns directly a value or an expression that must be evaluated. To transfer the return value to the caller, we save it in the Memory with the identifier '*return*'. The function call knows that, once the evaluation of the function is completed, the return value is stored in $N'_\rho(\rho'(\mathit{return}))$.

7) Function Call:

$$(\!| fname(e_1...e_n) |\!)\sigma \stackrel{\text{def}}{=} (\!| \text{BODY} |\!)\sigma' = \langle N'_\rho(\rho'(return)), \sigma'' \rangle$$

$$\text{where } \sigma' = \langle N'_\rho, \rho', C, A \rangle \text{ s.t. } N'_\rho = \{(fp_i \leftarrow l_i) \mid \forall i \in [1, n]\},$$
$$\rho' = \{(l_i \leftarrow (\!| e_i |\!)\sigma_{i-1}) \mid \forall i \in [1, n], \sigma_0 = \sigma\}$$
$$l_i \in \text{MLOC fresh and } \sigma'' = \langle N_\rho, \rho, C', A' \rangle$$

$$\text{BODY} = \begin{cases} \texttt{Pbody} = C(\dot{c}).\lambda.P(fname, \forall i \mid t_i) & \texttt{Pbody} \neq \bot \\ \texttt{Ibody} = C(\dot{c}).\lambda.I(fname, \forall i \mid t_i) & \texttt{Ibody} \neq \bot \\ \texttt{Ebody} = C(\dot{c}).\lambda.E(fname, \forall i \mid t_i) & \texttt{Ebody} \neq \bot \\ \texttt{Rbody} = C(\dot{c}).\lambda.R(fname, \forall i \mid t_i) & \texttt{Rbody} \neq \bot \end{cases}$$
$$\text{where } t_i = \text{type}((\!| e_i |\!)\sigma_{i-1})$$

The semantics of a function call corresponds to the execution result of the function body. In particular, the function body must be executed in a state taking into account of the parameters passed to the function call, memory σ'. Then C, A are unattached from σ while N'_ρ and ρ' contains all the associations between actual and formal parameters. The return instruction saves, as previously said, the final value in $N'_\rho(\rho'(return))$. This one is returned to the caller with the Storage modified by the last evaluation and the Memory that the caller had before the call.

8) Transfer: We have chosen to implement the `transfer` function. This is not the only way that exists to transfer ETH between addresses, but is the most secure. In fact, there are also the `call` function, that is now deprecated, and the `send` function that can be still used but, contrary to the `transfer` function, when it fails, it simply returns false and does not propagate the exception. This behaviour can lead to unwanted errors and vulnerabilities [6]. Regarding the way we implemented the transfer function, we choose not to handle the exceptions. We studied three possible results of transfers:

- A transfer is done between two contracts with a correct amount of ETH and no fallback function is invoked.
- A transfer is done between two contracts with a correct amount of ETH and a fallback function is invoked.
- A transfer is done between two contracts with an incorrect amount of ETH and this lead to an error.

$$(\!| \tilde{a}.\texttt{transfer}(\texttt{n}) |\!)\sigma \stackrel{\text{def}}{=} \sigma'$$

$$\sigma' = \begin{cases} \langle N_\rho, \rho, C, (A[\dot{c} \leftarrow A(\dot{c}) - n])[\tilde{a} \leftarrow A(\tilde{a}) + n] \rangle & \text{1st case} \\ \\ \langle N_\rho, \rho, C', A' \rangle \stackrel{\text{def}}{=} (\!| C(\tilde{a}).\lambda.E(\epsilon, \varnothing) |\!)\sigma'' \\ \mid \sigma'' = \langle N_\rho, \rho, C, A' \rangle & \text{2nd case} \\ \mid A' = (A[\dot{c} \leftarrow A(\dot{c}) - n])[\tilde{a} \leftarrow A(\tilde{a}) + n] \\ \\ exception & \text{3rd case} \end{cases}$$

$$\text{1st case} : A(\dot{c}) \geq n \wedge (C(\tilde{a}) = \bot \vee$$
$$(C(\tilde{a}) \neq \bot \wedge C(\tilde{a}).\lambda.E(\epsilon, \varnothing) = \bot))$$
$$\text{2nd case} : A(\dot{c}) \geq n \wedge C(\tilde{a}) \neq \bot \wedge C(\tilde{a}).\lambda.E(\epsilon, \varnothing) \neq \bot$$
$$\text{3rd case} : A(\dot{c}) < n$$

The three cases are described before. In the first and second case, we transfer the amount of ETH from $\dot{c}$ to $\tilde{a}$, but in the second case the recipient is also a contract, therefore the returned Memory depends on the execution of $\tilde{a}$ fallback function. In Figure 1 we propose a simple example of a contract that receives Ether and returns the full amount through the invocation of function `sendEther` when the contract balance is at least 0.3 ETH. The contract mentions the ***msg*** field that we have not covered in this core. It contains useful information of the transaction, e.g., the sender and, for ETH transfers, the amount sent.

V. Conclusion And Future Works

In this paper, we have introduced a Solidity core and a formal semantics for it. This required us to introduce a first concept of an abstract memory model, that is able to run the code on the EVM. This model is also able to represent blockchain and its complex structure and behaviour. In order to extend our work, the next step is to create a more complete and meaningful core by adding the missing constructs. In this way, we will be able to provide a better representation of the contracts on the blockchain. At this stage, our core is enough to give a first idea and can provide the semantics of only basic contracts. As a future work, we plan to build a static analyzer, based on abstract interpretation [7], for the smart contracts written in Solidity.

References

[1] K. Bhargavan et al., "Formal verification of smart contracts: Short paper," in Proceedings of the 2016 ACM Workshop on Programming Languages and Analysis for Security, PLAS@CCS 2016, Vienna, Austria, October 24, 2016, T. C. Murray and D. Stefan, Eds. ACM, 2016, pp. 91–96, URL: https://doi.org/10.1145/2993600.2993611 [accessed: 2019-10-22].

[2] B. K. Mohanta, S. S. Panda, and D. Jena, "An overview of smart contract and use cases in blockchain technology," in 2018 9th International Conference on Computing, Communication and Networking Technologies (ICCCNT), July 2018, pp. 1–4.

[3] J. Zakrzewski, "Towards verification of ethereum smart contracts: A formalization of core of solidity," in Verified Software. Theories, Tools, and Experiments - 10th International Conference, VSTTE 2018, Oxford, UK, July 18-19, 2018, Revised Selected Papers, ser. Lecture Notes in Computer Science, R. Piskac and P. Rümmer, Eds., vol. 11294. Springer, 2018, pp. 229–247.

[4] "Ethereum - Solidity documentation," 2019, URL: https://solidity.readthedocs.io/en/v0.5.10 [accessed: 2019-10-22].

[5] J. Jiao et al., "Executable operational semantics of solidity," CoRR, vol. abs/1804.01295, 2018, URL: http://arxiv.org/abs/1804.01295 [accessed: 2019-10-22].

[6] "King of the Ether Throne - Post-Mortem Investigation," 2016, URL: https://www.kingoftheether.com/postmortem.html [accessed: 2019-10-22].

[7] P. Cousot and R. Cousot, "Automatic synthesis of optimal invariant assertions: Mathematical foundations," SIGART Newsletter, vol. 64, 1977, pp. 1–12.

[8] S. Sahoo, A. M. Fajge, R. Halder, and A. Cortesi, "A hierarchical and abstraction-based blockchain model," Applied Sciences, vol. 9, no. 11, Jun. 2019, p. 2343, URL: http://dx.doi.org/10.3390/app9112343 [accessed: 2019-10-22].

Learning Metamorphic Rules from Widening Control Flow Graphs

Marco Campion
Dipartimento di Informatica
University of Verona
Verona, Italy
email:marco.campion@univr.it

Mila Dalla Preda
Dipartimento di Informatica
University of Verona
Verona, Italy
email:mila.dallapreda@univr.it

Roberto Giacobazzi
Dipartimento di Informatica
University of Verona
Verona, Italy
email:roberto.giacobazzi@univr.it

***Abstract*—Metamorphic malware are self-modifying programs which apply semantic preserving transformation rules to their own code in order to foil detection systems based on signature matching. Thus, a metamorphic malware is a malware equipped with a metamorphic engine that takes the malware, or parts of it, as input and morphs it at runtime to a syntactically different but semantically equivalent variant. Examples of code transformation rules used by the metamorphic engine are: dead code insertion, registers swap and substitution of small sequences of instructions with semantically equivalent ones. With the term metamorphic signature, we refer to an abstract program representation that ideally captures all the possible code variants that might be generated during the execution of a metamorphic program. In this paper, we consider the problem of automatically extracting metamorphic signatures from the analysis of metamorphic malware variants. For this purpose, we developed *MetaWDN*, a tool which takes as input a collection of simplified metamorphic code variants and extracts their control flow graphs. *MetaWDN* uses these graphs to build an approximated automaton, which over-approximates the considered code variants. Learning techniques are then applied in order to extract the code transformation rules used by the metamorphic engine to generate the considered code variants.**

Keywords*—*Static binary analysis; Metamorphic malware detection; Program semantics; Widening automata; Learning grammars.

I. Introduction

Detecting and neutralizing computer malware, such as worms, viruses, trojans, and spyware is a major challenge in modern computer security, involving both sophisticated intrusion detection strategies and advanced code manipulation tools and methods. Traditional misuse malware detectors (also known as signature-based detectors) are typically syntactic in nature: they use pattern matching to compare the byte sequence comprising the body of the malware against a signature database [1]. Malware writers have responded by using a variety of techniques in order to avoid detection: encryption, oligomorphism with mutational decryption patterns, and polymorphism with different encryption methods for generating an endless sequence of decryption patterns are typical strategies for achieving malware diversification.

Metamorphism emerged in the last decade as an effective alternative strategy to foil misuse malware detectors. Metamorphic malware are self-modifying programs which iteratively apply code transformation rules that preserve the semantics of programs. These code transformations change the syntax of code in order to foil detection systems based on signature matching. These programs are equipped with a metamorphic engine that usually represents the 90% of the whole program code. This engine takes as input the malware and its own code and it produces at run time a syntactically different but semantically equivalent program. We call metamorphic variant the program variants generated by the metamorphic engine. At the assembly level these semantic preserving transformation include: semantic-nop/junk insertion, code permutation, register swap and substitution of equivalent sequences of instructions [2] (see Figure 1).

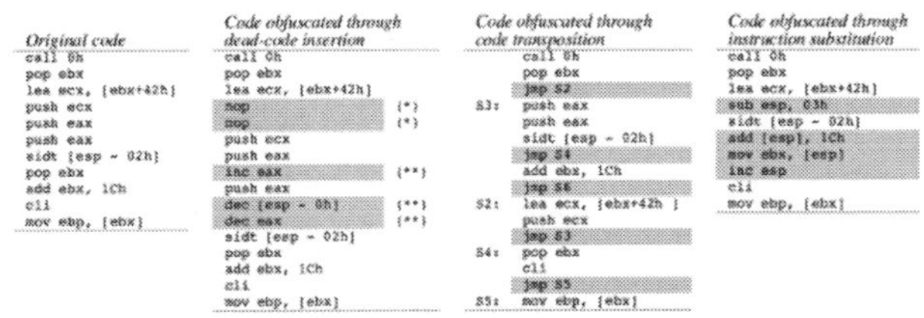

Figure 1. Examples of semantic preserving rules transformation.

The large amount of possible metamorphic variants makes it impractical to maintain a signature set that is large enough to cover most or all of these variants, thus making standard signature-based detection ineffective. Heuristic techniques, on the other side, may be prone to false positives or false negatives. The key to identify these type of malicious programs consists in considering semantic program features and not purely syntactic program features, thus capturing code mutations while preserving the semantic intent [6]. For this reason, we would like to capture those semantic aspects that allow us to detect all the possible variants that can be generated by the metamorphic engine. We use the term metamorphic signature to refer to an abstract program representation that ideally captures all the possible code variants that might be generated during the execution of a metamorphic program. A metamorphic signature is therefore any (possibly decidable) approximation of the properties of code evolution.

The goal of this work is to statically extract a so called metamorphic signature, i.e., a signature of the metamorphic engine itself. In this setting, a metamorphic signature consists of a set of rewriting rules that the malware can use to change its code. These rules are represented as a pure context-free grammar in which each instruction is a terminal symbol and can be transformed into equivalent instructions following a production of the grammar. For this purpose, we built a tool, called *MetaWDN*, that takes as input simplified versions of the metamorphic code variants, embeds them in an over-approximating control flow graph (*widening*) and finally, it tries to *learn* from the control flow graph the rewriting rules used to generate each variant. The general structure of the tool is represented in Figure 2.

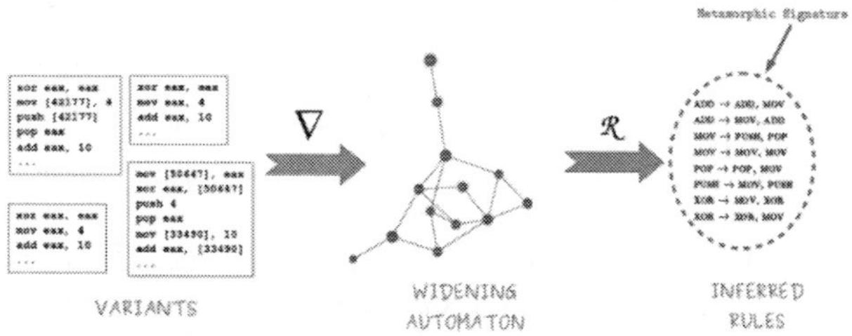

Figure 2. Capturing the metamorphic signature.

In order to test the quality of the output on portions of code that are actual metamorphic variants of the same program, we have implemented a metamorphic engine. Our metamorphic engine takes as inputs a program written in an intermediate language very similar to the `x86` assembly and it randomly chooses the rewriting rules to apply in order to generate the metamorphic variants. The metamorphic rules implemented are a subset of ones used by the metamorphic malware MetaPHOR [14]. The metamorphic engine allows us to quickly generate numerous test sets, input them to the tool and check the quality of the results by comparing the rules inferred with those actually applied by the metamorphic engine.

The rest of this paper is organized as follows: in Section II we discuss some related work, Section III explains how the tool can be executed and how it works, in Section IV we present some results and consideration applied to one example and finally the paper ends with conclusion and future work in Section V.

II. Related Work

In [3] the authors propose a malware detector scheme based on the detection of suspicious system call sequences. In particular, they consider only a reduction (subgraph) of the control flow graph of the program, which contains only the nodes that represent certain system calls and finally, they check if this subgraph has some known malicious system call sequences.

In [8] the authors describe a system of malware detection based on containment and unification of languages. The malicious code and the possible infected program are modeled as an automaton with unresolved symbols and placeholders for registers dealing with certain types of obfuscation. In this configuration, a program exhibits malicious behavior if the intersection between the malware's automaton language and the one of the program is not empty.

In [4] the authors specify malicious behavior through a Linear Temporal Logic (LTL) formula and then use the SPIN model checker to check if this property is satisfied by the control flow graph of a suspicious program.

In [5] the authors introduce a new Computation Tree Predicate Logic (CTPL) temporal logic, which is an extension of the logic CTL, which takes into account the quantification of the registers, allowing a natural presentation of malicious patterns.

In [9] they describe a malicious behavior model through a template, that is a generalization of the malicious code that expresses the malicious intent excluding the details of the implementation. The idea is that the template does not distinguish between irrelevant variants of the same malware obtained through obfuscation processes. For example, a template will use symbolic variables / constants to handle the renaming of variables and registers, and will be related to the malware control flow graph in order to handle code reordering. Finally, they propose an algorithm that checks if a program presents the behavior as a template, using a process of unification between the variables / constants of the program and the symbolic variables / constants of the malware.

In [7] Dalla Preda et al. consider the problem of automatically extracting metamorphic signatures from metamorphic code. They introduced a semantic for self-modifying code, called phase semantics, and prove its correctness by proving that it is an abstract interpretation of standard trace semantics. Phase semantics precisely models the metamorphic behavior of the code, providing a set of program traces which correspond to the possible evolution of the metamorphic code during execution. They therefore demonstrate that metamorphic signatures can be automatically extracted by abstract interpretation of phase semantics. In particular, they introduce the notion of regular metamorphism, in which the invariants of phase semantics can be modeled as a Finite State Automata (FSA) representing the code structure of all possible metamorphic changes of a metamorphic code.

In [10], the authors propose to model the behavior of a metamorphic engine of a malicious program, with rewriting systems also called term-rewriting systems and to formalize the problem of constructing a normalizer for rewrite systems (called NCP) that is able to reduce to the same normal form, variants of malware generated by the same metamorphic engine. From this problem, they propose a possible solution by building a normalizer on a set of rules that maintain three properties: termination, confluence and preservation of equivalence.

All these approaches provide a model of the metamorphic behavior that is based on the knowledge of the metamorphic transformations, i.e., obfuscations, that malware typically use. By knowing how the code mutates, it is possible to specify suitable (semantics-based) equivalence relations which trace code evolution and detect malware. This knowledge is typically the result of a time and cost consuming tracking analysis, based on emulation and heuristics, which requires intensive human interaction in order to achieve an abstract specification of code features that are common to the malware variants obtained through various obfuscations and mutations.

In this paper, we aim at defining an automatic technique for the extraction of a metamorphic signature that does not need any a priori knowledge of the code transformation rules used by the metamorphic engine.

III. *MetaWDN* TOOL

MetaWDN is a program written in *Python 3* language that allows us to automatically generate a set of variants starting from a given input program. Next, *MetaWDN* compacts them all together through the widening operator and then it tries to automatically derive the rewriting rules used to generate them. Depending on the execution parameters, the tool can be executed in one of the following ways (Figure 3):

- execution of the metamorphic engine to generate a desired number of variants starting from a set of instructions (which will be the starting program) written on an input text file (①);
- computing the widening between a set of variants given as inputs in order to build an unique abstract representation of the considered metamorphic variants (②);
- inferring the rewriting rules from the program representation obtained through the widening process (② → ③);
- finally, you can run all the operation above (① → ② → ③).

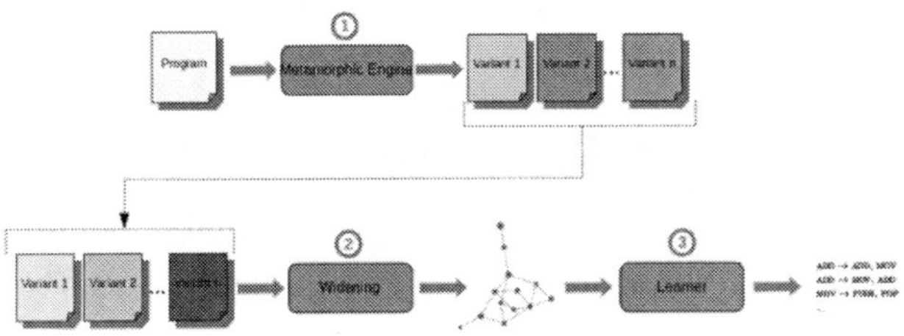

Figure 3. Phase of execution of *MetaWDN*.

The tool takes as input programs written in an intermediate language very similar to the language used by MetaPHOR [14], both with the aim of simplifying and abstracting the `x86` assembly language. Therefore, the input is an extremely simplified version compared to the code that can be found in any executable. You can use the classic instructions of the `x86` assembly code with *Intel* syntax like: data manipulation (`mov, push, pop, lea`), mathematical expressions (`add, sub, and, xor, or`), jumps (`je, jne, jl, jle, jg, jge, jmp, call`), etc. There are three kinds of operands: registers (`eax, ebx, ecx, edx, esp, ebp, esi, edi`), immediate values and memory values (decimal number or register between square brackets, for example `[77382]`). For jump instructions, the memory value to which the instruction can jump corresponds to the line number where the target instruction is located (the first line starts from zero). Analogously, for function calls we have that in the instruction `call` the value of the operand corresponds to the line number of the first statement of the function. Each function (including function `main`) must end with the instruction `ret`.

A. *The Metamorphic Engine*

The tool can be executed as a metamorphic engine: it takes as input a text file containing a program written in the `x86` intermediate language and the number of variants to be generated. The implemented rewriting rules are instructions transformation that preserve the semantics, e.g., `mov` → `push, pop` which expands the instruction `mov` in two instructions `push` and `pop`. A rewriting rule could be applied either in expansion (following the rule from left to right) or in reduction (right to left). After reading the file, the metamorphic engine randomly selects: the rewriting rule to apply, the line of the program where to apply the rule, and whether to apply the rule as expansion or reduction. If it is not possible to apply the rewriting rule to the selected instruction, the following instruction is considered and if it is not possible to apply the rule to the whole file then another rewriting rule is selected randomly. The implemented rewriting rules are a subset of the rules used by the `MetaPHOR` metamorphic engine [14].

B. *Widening Control Flow Graphs*

Each metamorphic variant is represented as a Control Flow Graph (CFG). Each node of the CFG contains one instruction that is abstracted according to an abstraction function that removes details usually modified by the metamorphic transformations. In particular, *MetaWDN* abstracts instructions by eliminating the operands, so, e.g., the instruction `mov eax, 4` is abstracted in `mov`. In the CFG representation of programs the vertices contain the instructions to be executed, and the edges represent possible control flow. For our purposes, it is convenient to consider a dual representation where vertices correspond to program locations and abstract instructions label edges. The resulting representation is isomorphic to FSA over an alphabet of instructions [13]. For this reason we use the terms CFG and automaton interchangeably. In order to compact the CFG of the metamorphic variants into an unique representation we use a widening operator. This allows us to obtain an unique representation that contains all the seen metamorphic varinats but that also generalizes the considered mutations. Given the equivalence between CFG and FSA, we can use the widening operator for FSA defined in [13]. To this end, we have to to compute the language of each node of the CFG. According to [13], we define the language of length `N` of a node of a CFG as the set of all the strings of length less or equal than `N` that are reachable from the considered node.

Example III.1. Consider the following program P, where the numbers on the left correspond to line numbers:

```
0: mov eax, 1       4: jmp 1
1: cmp eax, 1000    5: ret
2: jge 5            6: add eax, 1
3: call 6           7: ret
```

the CFG is represented in Figure 4. The alphabet of the

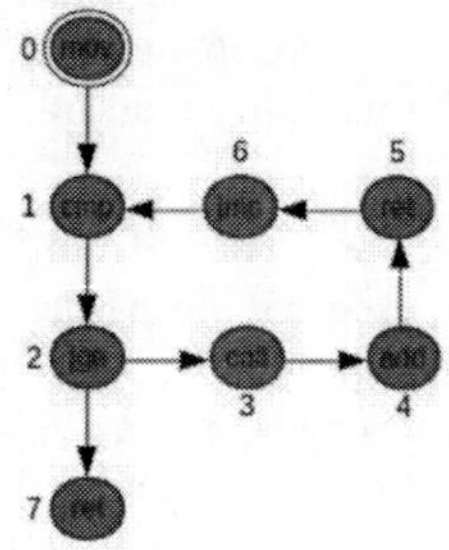

Figure 4. CFG of Example III.1.

CFG of P is {mov, cmp, jge, call, jmp, add, ret}, and the language of length 2 recognized by the nodes is:

```
lang(0)  = {(mov),(mov,cmp)}
lang(1)  = {(cmp),(cmp,jge)}
lang(2)  = {(jge),(jge,call),(jge,ret)}
lang(3)  = {(call),(call,add)}
lang(4)  = {(add),(add,ret)}
lang(5)  = {(ret),(ret,jmp)}
lang(6)  = {(jmp),(jmp,cmp)}
lang(7)  = {(ret)}
```

Consider a set of code variants $V_1V_2 \ldots V_n$ generated from the initial program P. The widening operator ∇ is defined as:

$$W_0 = \alpha(P) \qquad W_{i+1} = W_i \underset{k}{\nabla}(W_i \cup \alpha(V_i))$$

where W_i with $i \geqslant 0$ is the widening CFG at step i (the initial widening W_0 is the CFG of the program itself), α is the abstraction function that eliminates the operands of instructions, and k is the length of the language of nodes. Briefly, the widening operator merges all the nodes with the same language of length k.

C. *Learning Rewriting Rules*

The section of the tool that infers the transformation rules is called learner. The learning algorithm implemented in *MetaWDN* is a simplified version of the algorithm proposed in [16] for learning pure grammars from a set of words. The general problem of inferring rewriting rules from a set of positive examples, i.e., from a positive set, can be transformed into the general problem of inferring a grammar starting from a set of strings belonging to a language. In particular, we try to infer a grammar that is able to generate at least all the strings given as input to the algorithm and belonging to the language to be studied. In our case, the language to be learned includes all the possible variants generated by the unknown metamorphic engine, while the grammar we want to infer corresponds to the set of rewriting rules used by the metamorphic engine to generate the metamorphic variants given in input to the positive set. Pure grammars [11] have been chosen as a formal representation for the rewriting rules, because they do not present terminal symbols but all the symbols are considered as non-terminals. In fact, the metamorphic transformation rules are all instructions of the same type, that is, they can be transformed into other instructions by applying the correct production. More in details, since the general problem of learning pure grammars from a positive set is undecidable [12], we move to the formalism of k-uniform pure context-free grammars [11] where, each production has the left part with one letter of the alphabet while the right part has at most k symbols of the alphabet. All these restrictions, of course, will lead to a loss of precision in the rules inferred by the tool as it will only be possible to infer productions of the form $\{x \rightarrow y \mid |x| = 1, |y| \leqslant k\}$. In our learning algorithm, the constant k is always set to 2 since the rewriting rules implemented in the tool have the right part of length 2. The learning algorithm takes a CFG as input and operates in three phases:

1. it builds the positive set;
2. it learns the rewriting rules;
3. finally, it eliminates the spurious inferred rules.

The positive set consists of a set of code variants where all the instructions are abstracted (no operands). This set is built in the widening phase and will be the input for inferring the rewriting rules. The length min of the smallest variant is calculated, i.e., the variant with the fewest instructions. Then, all the paths of length min of the graph that go from a root node (the first instruction of a variant, those drawn with the double circle) to the final node (the ret instruction) are visited. For each path found, the set of instructions related to the visited nodes are inserted in the positive set. During this process every time that we visit an edge we mark it. When the path of length min has been found, if all the edges are marked then the search is interrupted without visiting other paths. Otherwise the variable min is incremented.

Given a couple of code variants (V_i, V_j) with $|V_i| < |V_j|$, the idea of the learning algorithm is to add a production rule r of the form $V_i \xrightarrow{r} V_j$. The rewriting rule r is inferred through simplification rules between the two variants (V_i, V_j). There are three kinds of simplification rules:

- top simplification: compare the first instruction of V_i and V_j and delete them if they are the same. This process continues until two different instructions are encountered: in this case, if $|V_i| > 1$ then the comparison restarts from the last instruction of V_i and V_j, otherwise ($|V_i| = 1$) the rule is added to the set of inferred rules;
- bottom simplification: it is similar to the previous one, but starts from the last instruction;
- top and bottom simplification: compare the first instruction of V_i and V_j and, if they are equal, it deletes them and starts again but from the bottom instruction of V_i and V_j.

The algorithm applies the top simplification repeatedly until a rule is added to the set of inferred rules and then it starts back with bottom simplification and finally, with top and bottom simplification.

Example III.2. Let us consider the following simple code variants: xor, mov, push and xor, push, pop, push. After applying two times the top simplification we get

~~xor~~,mov,~~push~~ → ~~xor~~,push,pop,~~push~~

Since the left part is of length 1 then the rule mov → push,pop is added to the set of inferred rules. With the other two kinds of simplification we get the same rewriting rule.

After the simplification phase, the algorithm has produced a set of rewriting rules of the form: $\{x \to y \mid |x| = 1, |y| \leqslant k\}$. However, most of these rules are superfluous since they can be generated by other rules of the set. The elimination algorithm tries to reduce the right part of each rewriting rule by applying all rewriting rules inferred in the reduction form (from right to left). If at the end of this procedure, the rule is reduced to another rule already in the inferred set, then that rule can be eliminated.

Example III.3. Let us suppose that there are two rewriting rules inferred by the learning algorithm:

1) mov → mov,mov

2) mov → push,pop

Now suppose that the following rewriting rule is produced: mov → push,pop,mov,mov. This rule is spurious since:

$$\text{push,pop,}\underline{\text{mov,mov}} \stackrel{1)}{\Rightarrow} \underline{\text{push,pop}}\text{,mov} \stackrel{2)}{\Rightarrow} \text{mov,mov}$$

IV. Case Studies

In the following section, we present some results and considerations applied to a program of 21 instructions:

```
0: mov [ebp], [esp]    11: mov eax, ebx
1: sub ebp, 4          12: push eax
2: push 100            13: pop [440303]
3: pop ecx             14: pop [443905]
4: cmp eax, exc        15: xor eax, 0
5: xor eax, 0          16: xor eax, eax
6: test eax, eax       17: nop
7: mov eax, 4          18: test eax, 0
8: sub eax, 1          19: xor eax, 0
9: cmp eax, ebx        20: ret
10: nop
```

We have used *MetaWDN* to generate 50 variants of this program. Next we have randomly selected a subset of 25 code variants that are obtained by applying all the rewriting rules implemented in *MetaWDN*. This subset is provided as input to the widening process (with language length sets to 2) and next to the learning process. The final graph of the widening is shown in the Figure 5. The rewriting rules inferred by the tool is the empty set. This looks like a mistake, however, by looking more carefully at the possible paths of the graph we observe that all paths from any root node to the `ret` node, starting from the minimum length (the smallest variant in terms of instructions), are already visited. For this reason, the set of positive examples contains all code variants of the same length and therefore it is not possible to infer any rewriting rule. This result is caused by the numerous spurious variants inserted by the widening process that agglomerates the nodes with the same language of length 2. In fact, due to

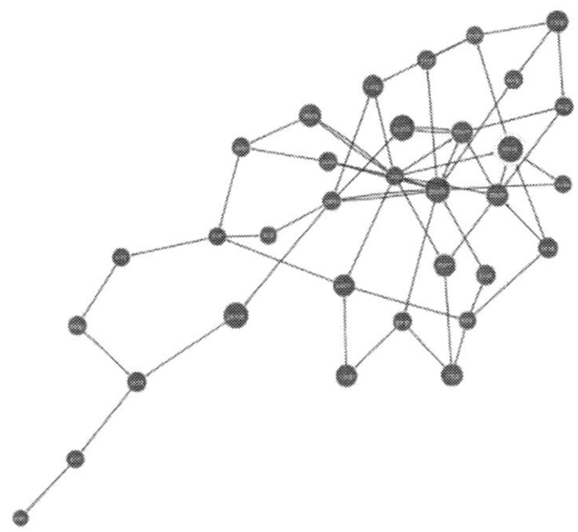

Figure 5. Graph obtained by the widening operator with length sets to 2.

the numerous cycles, i.e., regularities inserted by the widening, a path from the root to the end node of length less than any true variant is "increased" until reaching the minimum length (in this example equal to 20) thus creating a spurious variant.

If we increase the level of precision of the widening by setting the parameter of the language length to 3, we obtain the graph in Figure 6 with the following rewriting rules inferred:

```
cmp -> ['cmp', 'mov']      mov -> ['push', 'mov']
mov -> ['push', 'pop']     mov -> ['mov', 'push']
mov -> ['pop', 'mov']      nop -> ['pop', 'push']
nop -> ['pop', 'mov']      nop -> ['nop', 'mov']
pop -> ['pop', 'push']     pop -> ['pop', 'mov']
pop -> ['mov', 'pop']      pop -> ['nop', 'mov']
push -> ['mov', 'push']    sub -> ['mov', 'sub']
test -> ['test', 'mov']    xor -> ['mov', 'xor']
```

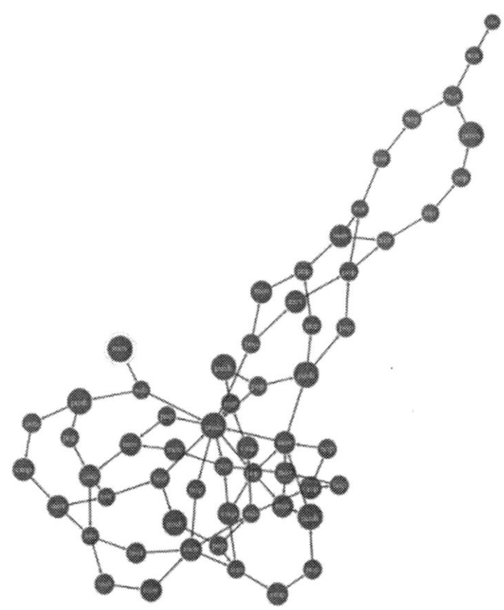

Figure 6. Graph obtained by the widening operator with length sets to 3.

Clearly, by increasing the length of the widening language we obtain a graph with more nodes but more precise. In fact, in this case it is possible to infer the rewriting rules even if there are numerous spurious rules still due to the presence of spurious paths induced by the widening.

If we increase the level of precision of the widening, setting the length of the language to 4 we obtain the following rewriting rules inferred:

```
cmp -> ['cmp', 'mov']       cmp -> ['mov', 'cmp']
mov -> ['push', 'pop']      mov -> ['mov', 'mov']
nop -> ['nop', 'mov']       nop -> ['pop', 'push']
pop -> ['pop', 'mov']       pop -> ['mov', 'pop']
push -> ['mov', 'push']     sub -> ['mov', 'sub']
test -> ['test', 'mov']     xor -> ['mov', 'xor']
```

Thanks to the greater precision of the widening, this time the inferred rules are more precise and they represent an acceptable result. Moreover, with a language length equal to 5 the same rules are still obtained.

V. Conclusion and Future Work

In this work we tried to capture the behavior of the metamorphic engine itself, namely we tried to find a set of rules that allow us to predict possible mutations of code variants starting from a set of examples. To this end, we presented the tool *MetaWDN* that has three main functions: metamorphic engine, widening of code variants and learning of rewriting rules. Thanks to the metamorphic engine, it is possible to quickly generate numerous variants in an intermediate language similar to `x86`. These variants are created by randomly applying rewriting rules implemented in the tool. The goal is to capture, starting from a subset of these code variants, the rewriting rules used by the metamorphic engine to generate them. Starting from the set of code variants, *MetaWDN* uses a widening operator to generate a graph that approximates all the variants of the set. Rewriting rules are then represented as productions of a k-uniform pure context-free grammar. From the learning algorithm and the elimination of superfluous rewriting rules algorithm, it is possible to obtain a set of rules that describes, in an approximate way, the possible evolution of code variants. The experimental results show us how the choice of the language length parameter of the widening operator affects the precision of the learned rules. The lower the value is, the more the nodes will be joined together because they will be more likely to present the same language. In this case the presence of spurious paths will be higher therefore there will be less precision in the results inferred by the learner. On the contrary, the higher the length of the language is and the greater is the precision of the graph. This means that the widening graph presents fewer spurious paths and therefore it allows us to infer more precise rewriting rules. Of course, the increase in precision comes at a cost in terms of time execution and memory consumption.

As a priority of future work, we will try to apply this tool to a set of real malware variants. In this work only one level of abstraction on the instructions has been considered, that is, the one that does not consider the operands. It would be interesting to consider different abstractions, assigning, for example, to the operands symbolic values such as those of [15]. Finally, an implementation of new rewriting rules in the tool and a new learner should be considered as a future work. The new learner needs to be able to learn, in an approximate way, more complex rewriting rules in order to catch more sophisticated metamorphic engine.

Acknowledgment

This paper has been supported by the grant PRIN2017 (code: 201784YSZ5) by MIUR Italy.

References

[1] P. Szr, "The Art of Computer Virus Research and Defense", Addison-Wesley Professional, Boston, MA, USA, 2005.

[2] D. Bruschi, L. Martignoni, and M. Monga, "Code normalization for self-mutating malware", IEEE Security and Privacy, vol. 5, no. 2, pp. 4654, 2007.

[3] J. Bergeron, M. Debbabi, J. Desharnais, M. Erhioui, Y. Lavoie, and N. Tawbi, "Static detection of malicious code in executable programs", Symposium on Requirements Engineering for Information Security, vo. 2001, no. 79, pp. 184-189, 2001.

[4] P. Singh, and A. Lakhotia, "Static verification of worm and virus behaviour in binary executables using model checking", IEEE Systems, Man and Cybernetics Society Information Assurance Workshop, pp. 298-300, 2003.

[5] J. Kinder, S. Katzenbeisser, C. Schallhart, and H. Veith, "Detecting malicious code by model checking", International Conference on Detection of Intrusions and Malware, and Vulnerability Assessment, pp. 174-187, 2005.

[6] M. Dalla Preda, "The grand challenge in metamorphic analysis", International Conference on Information Systems, Technology and Management, vol. 285, pp. 439-444, 2012.

[7] M. Dalla Preda, R. Giacobazzi, and S. Debray, "Unveiling metamorphism by abstract interpretation of code properties", Theoretical Computer Science, vo. 577, pp. 74-97, 2015.

[8] M. Christodorescu and S. Jha, "Static analysis of executables to detect malicious patterns", Symposium on USENIX Security, 2003.

[9] M. Christodorescu, S. Jha, S. A. Seshia, D. Song, and R. E. Bryant, "Semantics-aware malware detection", IEEE Symposium on Security and Privacy, pp. 32-46, 2005.

[10] A. Walestein, R. Mathur, M. R. Chouchane, and A. Lakhotia, "Constructing malware normalizers using term rewriting", Journal in Computer Virology, vo. 4, no. 4, pp. 307-322, 2008.

[11] H. A. Maurer, A. Salornaa, and D. Wood, "Pure grammars", Inform. Control, vo. 44, pp. 47-72, 1980.

[12] T. Koshiba, E. Mkinen, and Y. Takada, "Inferring pure context-free languages from positive data", Journal in Acta Cybernetica, vo. 14, no. 3, pp. 469-477, 2000.

[13] V. D'Silva, "Widening for automata", Diploma thesis, Institut Fur Informatick, Universitat Zurich, 2006.

[14] P. Beaucamps, "Advanced Metamorphic Techniques in Computer Viruses", International Conference on Computer, Electrical, Systems Science, and Engineering, 2007.

[15] A. Lakhotia, M. Dalla Preda, and R. Giacobazzi, "Fast location of similar code fragments using semantic Juice", In PPREW@ POPL, 2013.

[16] C. Higuera, "Grammatical inference: learning automata and grammars", Cambridge University Press, 2010.

Chameleon: The Gist of Dynamic Programming Languages

Samuele Buro
Dept. of Computer Science
University of Verona
Email: samuele.buro@univr.it

Michele Pasqua
Dept. of Computer Science
University of Verona
Email: michele.pasqua@univr.it

Isabella Mastroeni
Dept. of Computer Science
University of Verona
Email: isabella.mastroeni@univr.it

Abstract—**Dynamic programming languages, such as JavaScript and PHP, are widespread and heavily used. They provide very useful "dynamic" features, like run-time type inference, dynamic method calls, and built-in dynamic data structures. This makes it hard to build static analyzers, for automatic errors discovery. Yet, exploiting harmful behaviors in such programs, especially in web applications, can have significant impacts. In this paper, we present Chameleon, a core programming language summarizing the main features of the dynamic programming paradigm. Chameleon can be useful in defining, testing and comparing static analyses, aiming at preventing bugs and errors in programs written in dynamic programming languages. With Chameleon, static analysis experts could define and test control mechanisms without the burden to take in consideration the technical details characterizing a specific real-world programming language.**

Keywords–Programming language design; Dynamic programming languages; Program static analysis.

I. Introduction

In the last years, dynamic programming languages, such as JavaScript or PHP, exponentially enhanced their popularity and nowadays are deeply used in a very wide range of applications. For instance, JavaScript is the *de facto* standard for client-side web programming, while, on the server-side, PHP, Python, and Ruby are the most common used languages. This success is mainly due to the several features that such languages provide to developers, making the writing of programs easier and faster.

Although there is no black and white distinction between static and dynamic programming languages, the latter basically follows two main paradigms: The first, justifying also the adjective *dynamic*, is the lack of a *static* type system. Dynamic programming languages still have types, but they are checked at run-time, rather than compile-time. The absence of strict static checks promotes the second aspect of dynamic languages, namely a greater flexibility at run-time. The basic idea is that operations which may be statically forbidden or not expressible in other languages should be allowed and given some semantics, and the program execution should continue whenever possible.

The benefit of these design choices is that programmers have a high flexibility in writing code. The downside is that errors occur at run-time and little or no information is available for developer tools to prevent these errors statically. A static analyzer is a tool which abstractly executes the program, *i.e.*, approximates all its possible behaviors. The computed approximation is then used to detect bugs or to provide useful information to developer tools. Examples of static analysis comprise data-flow analysis [1], invariants analysis [2] and model-checking [3].

Due to the dynamic nature of these languages, it is, indeed, very hard for static analysis experts to develop such control mechanisms. In addition to the aforementioned issues, there is the *heterogeneity* problem: it is not necessarily the case that an analysis designed for a programming language works also for the others.

Many authors [4]–[6] define their own toy language, in order to present the analysis they are introducing or improving. This is surely a burden for authors and, more importantly, it does not allow comparisons between similar static analyses, since the underling language is different.

To overcome these issues, we propose a core programming language, called *Chameleon* (also typesetted as ©hameleon), summarizing the main features of dynamic programming languages. It abstracts the implementation details characterizing each language, allowing to focus on the analysis of the dynamic features only. Indeed, building static analyzers for real programming languages is a very complex and time-consuming engineering task. Having a simple language, yet sufficiently expressive to model the main dynamic features, allows to define new static analyses faster and easier.

Furthermore, Chameleon could be used as a common ground for the definition and comparison, of static analysis techniques, aiming at reasoning about programs written in dynamic programming languages, without being restricted to a particular language. Ideally, when an analysis has been sufficiently tested on Chameleon, then it could be ported to the target *real-world* programming language with just engineering efforts and without losing theoretical solidity.

Outline: In Section II we describe the Chameleon language, first its syntax (Subsection II-A) and then its semantics (Subsection II-B). Finally, we draw conclusions, in Section III.

II. The ©hameleon Language

Chameleon is a programming language designed specifically to ease the definition of static analyses, with the focus on dynamic features of programming languages. Its core consists in a classic imperative language with assignments, conditionals and iterative constructs. This latter is extended with *functions/procedures* and with *non-determinism*. Non-determinism is modeled by means of an input construct, allowing programs to receive input values during execution. Chameleon is equipped with standard basic values (booleans, integers, rationals and strings), as well as inductive data-structures, such as *finite lists* of values and *finite dictionaries* (*i.e.*, identifier-value associations).

$\langle prog \rangle$ ::= $\overline{\langle fundef \rangle}_{;}$ $\langle com \rangle$
$\langle fundef \rangle$ ::= `function` $\langle id \rangle$ `(` $\overline{\langle exp \rangle}_{,}$ `)` `{` $\langle com \rangle$ `}`
$\langle com \rangle$ ::=
| `skip`
| $\langle id \rangle$ `:=` $\langle exp \rangle$
| $\langle id \rangle$ `[` $\langle exp \rangle$ `]` `:=` $\langle exp \rangle$
| `if` $\langle exp \rangle$ `then` `{` $\langle com \rangle$ `}` `else` `{` $\langle com \rangle$ `}`
| `while` $\langle exp \rangle$ `do` `{` $\langle com \rangle$ `}`
| $\langle com \rangle$ `;` $\langle com \rangle$
| `return` $\langle exp \rangle$
| $\langle exp \rangle$
$\langle exp \rangle$ ::=
| `(` $\langle exp \rangle$ `)`
| $\langle value \rangle$
| $\langle id \rangle$
| $\langle id \rangle$ `(` $\overline{\langle value \rangle}_{,}$ `)`
| $\langle exp \rangle$ `[` $\langle exp \rangle$ `]`
| `(` $\langle type \rangle$ `)` $\langle exp \rangle$
| `eval` $\langle exp \rangle$
| `input()`
| `size` `(` $\langle exp \rangle$ `)`
| `concat` `(` $\langle exp \rangle$ `,` $\langle exp \rangle$ `)`
| `charat` `(` $\langle exp \rangle$ `,` $\langle exp \rangle$ `)`
| `substr` `(` $\langle exp \rangle$ `,` $\langle exp \rangle$ `,` $\langle exp \rangle$ `)`
| `not` $\langle exp \rangle$
| `-` `(` $\langle exp \rangle$ `)`
| $\langle exp \rangle$ $\langle bop \rangle$ $\langle exp \rangle$
$\langle bop \rangle$ ::= `*` | `/` | `+` | `-` | `<=` | `>=` | `<` | `>` | `==` | `not` | `and` | `or`
$\langle type \rangle$ ::= `bool` | `int` | `rat` | `str`
| `[]`
| `[` $\overline{\langle type \rangle}_{,}$ `]`
| `[` $\overline{\langle id : type \rangle}_{,}$ `]`
$\langle value \rangle$ ::=
| $\bot$
| $b \in \mathbb{B}$
| $i \in \mathbb{Z}$
| $q \in \mathbb{Q}$
| $s \in \mathbb{S}$
| $\langle collection \rangle$
$\langle collection \rangle$ ::= `[]` | `[` $\overline{\langle exp \rangle}_{,}$ `]` | `[` $\overline{\langle id : exp \rangle}_{,}$ `]`
$\langle id \rangle$ ::= $x \in \mathbb{X}$

Figure 1. The syntax of Chameleon

Concerning properly dynamic features, Chameleon is *not statically typed* and it applies *type coercion* when needed. The language has a (limited) reflection mechanism, implemented with an *eval* construct. Finally, Chameleon expressions can have *side-effects*.

A. Syntax

The syntax of Chameleon is specified by the context-free grammar depicted in Figure 1. A *program* $P \in \langle prog \rangle$ is a list of *function definitions* $f \in \overline{\langle fundef \rangle}_{;}$ followed by a *command* $c \in \langle com \rangle$, which in turn can be a standard statement of an imperative language (like, in order, the do-nothing command, the assignment of a variable, a list element, or a field, the conditional statement, the conditional loop, and the composition), a return statement (which can be used either to leave the execution of a function with a value or to terminate the program when employed outside of functions body), or an *expression* $e \in \langle exp \rangle$.

An *expression* e in Chameleon is inductively defined by the syntactic category $\langle exp \rangle$. Its smallest building block are *identifiers* $x \in \langle id \rangle = \mathbb{X} = \{\texttt{a}, \texttt{b}, \dots, \texttt{z}\}^*$, and *simple values* which consist of the undefined value $\bot$, the *booleans* $b \in \mathbb{B} = \{\texttt{true}, \texttt{false}\}$, the *integers* $i \in \mathbb{Z}$, the *floats* $q \in \mathbb{Q}$, the *strings* $s \in \mathbb{S}$ (a string of the language is a sequence of characters over the alphanumeric alphabet enclosed by double quotes, *e.g.*, , "foo", "bar", etc., and we assume the Java-like syntax for characters escaping), and the empty list `[]`. Compound expressions are built inductively: If e is an expression, then (e) is a parenthesized expression; If $e_0, \dots, e_n$ and $x_0, \dots, x_n$ are a sequence of expressions and a sequence of identifiers, respectively, then $[e_0, \dots, e_n]$ is a non-empty list and $[x_0 : e_0, \dots, x_n : e_n]$ is a dictionary; If $f \in \mathbb{X}$ is a function name, then $f(e_0, \dots, e_n)$ is a function call with actual parameters $e_0, \dots, e_n \in \langle exp \rangle$, whereas $f()$ is a function call with no arguments; If $c \in \langle collection \rangle$ is a list or a dictionary (*i.e.*, a *collection*), then $c[e]$ is the access of an element in c, namely, a list access or a field access depending on the nature of c; If t is a type, then $(t)\ e$ is a cast to the type t. The rest of the rules of the grammar are self-explanatory and their purpose can be easily recovered by the semantic rules given in the next section. Briefly, they include the `eval` statement, the `input()` function, and several operators for the most common operations between values (the precedence rules for the binary operators in $\langle bop \rangle$ are the standard ones, and the associativity is always left to right).

In the following, we refer to the *set of all terms* $\mathcal{T}$ defined as the union of the sets of terms generated by each syntactic category of the Chameleon grammar.

B. Semantics

In this section, we formally describe the operational semantics of Chameleon. We start by defining the concepts of *ground values*, *types*, and *state* during an arbitrary step of computation, then we provide a *small-step operational semantics*.

1) Ground Values and Types: Let $\mathbb{V}$ be the set of *ground values* (with metavariable v) inductively defined as the smallest set such that $\{\bot\} \cup \mathbb{B} \cup \mathbb{Z} \cup \mathbb{Q} \cup \mathbb{S} \cup \{[]\} \subseteq \mathbb{V}$, and if $v_0, \dots, v_n \in \mathbb{V}$ and $x_0, \dots, x_n \in \mathbb{X}$, then $[v_0, \dots, v_n]$ and $[x_0 : v_0, \dots, x_n : v_n]$ belong to $\mathbb{V}$. Moreover, we define the set $\mathbb{C} = \mathbb{L} \cup \mathbb{D}$ of *ground collections*, where $\mathbb{L} = \{ l \in \mathbb{V} \mid l = [v_0, \dots, v_n] \} \cup \{[]\}$ of *ground lists* and the set $\mathbb{D} = \{ d \in \mathbb{V} \mid d = [x_0 : v_0, \dots, x_n : v_n] \}$ of *ground dictionaries.*

The type of a value is inductively defined by the function $\tau\colon \mathbb{V} \to \langle type \rangle_{\bot}$ as follows (see the previous section for the meaning of the metavariables employed in the definition): $\tau(\bot) = \bot$, $\tau(b) = \texttt{bool}$, $\tau(i) = \texttt{int}$, $\tau(f) = \texttt{rat}$, and $\tau(s) = \texttt{str}$. Moreover, if $l = [v_1, \dots, v_n]$ is a (potentially empty) ground list, then $\tau(l) = [\tau(v_1), \dots, \tau(v_n)]$ is the type of l, and if $d = [x_0 : v_0, \dots, x_n : v_n]$ is a ground dictionary, then $\tau(d) = [x_0 : \tau(v_0), \dots, x_n : \tau(v_n)]$ is the type of d. If $t, t' \in \tau(\mathbb{D})$, we define the equivalence relation $t \sim t'$ if and only if t' is a permutation of t.

In the following, we refer to $\bot$, `bool`, `int`, `rat`, and `str` as *simple types*, and to the other as *compound types*. Moreover, if

$t = [t_0, \dots, t_n]$ or $t = [x_0 : t_0, \dots, x_n : t_n]$ is a compound type, we define the length of t as $|t| = n+1$, and if $t = []$ then $|t| = 0$. Finally, we define the partial order relation $\preccurlyeq$ between types: $\bot \preccurlyeq t \preccurlyeq t$ for each type t, and bool $\preccurlyeq$ int $\preccurlyeq$ rat $\preccurlyeq$ str; if $t = [t_1, \dots, t_n]$ and $t' = [t'_0, \dots, t'_n]$, then $t \preccurlyeq t'$ if and only if $t_i \preccurlyeq t'_i$ for each $i = 0 \dots n$; If $t = [x_0 : t_0, \dots, x_n : t_n]$ and $t' = [x_0 : t'_0, \dots, x_n : t'_n]$, then $t \preccurlyeq t'$ if and only if $t_i \preccurlyeq t'_i$ for each $i = 0 \dots n$ or there are $\hat{t}$ and $\hat{t}'$ such that $t \sim \hat{t} \preccurlyeq \hat{t}' \sim t'$.

2) State: Let $\Sigma = \mathbb{X} \to \mathbb{V}$ be the set of *environments*, and let $\mathrm{P} = \mathbb{X} \to \left(\bigcup_{n \in \mathbb{N}} \mathbb{X}^n \times \langle com \rangle\right)_\bot$ be the set of *function definitions maps*. The *state* of the language during an arbitrary step of computation is an element of the set $\Pi = \Sigma^+ \times \Sigma \times \mathrm{P}$. Given $\pi = (\dot{\sigma}, \gamma, \rho) \in \Pi$, where $\dot{\sigma} = \sigma_0 \dots \sigma_n$, the second component γ denotes the *global state* (*i.e.*, the variables accessible throughout the program, unless shadowed by local ones), and $\dot{\sigma}$ is a non-empty list of *local states*. Intuitively, the list $\dot{\sigma}$ of local states shall be used to handle the scope of variables during a chain of function calls: Every time a function is called, a new component $\sigma \in \Sigma$ is appended to $\dot{\sigma}$, and new bindings between formal and actual parameters are created in σ. Conversely, every time a return statement is reached, the last component σ_n of $\dot{\sigma}$ is dropped, and the previous bindings are automatically restored. Moreover, the third component ρ in π serves to keep track of all the functions declared by a program. For instance, the following function

```
function factorial(n) {
    if (n < 2) then { return 1 };
    return n * factorial(n - 1)
}
```

is stored in ρ as $\rho(\texttt{factorial}) = (\texttt{n}, c)$, where c is the body of the function.

In order to handle the state in the small-step rules of the language, we define some compact notations that will be used throughout the paper: We write $\sigma = \{x_1 \mapsto v_1, \dots, x_n \mapsto v_n\}$ to define the environment $\sigma \in \mathbb{X} \to \mathbb{V}$ such that $\sigma(x) = v_i$ if $x = x_i$ for some $i = 1 \dots n$ and $\sigma(x) = \bot$ otherwise. Note that, unlike dictionaries, environments can be infinite objects as well as completely undefined (*i.e.*, when $n = 0$ and therefore $\sigma = \{\ \}$, then $\sigma(x) = \bot$ for all identifiers x). Moreover, if $\sigma \in \Sigma$, we denote the *update* of the variable x in σ with a value v as the new environment $\sigma[x \hookleftarrow v]$ defined as

$$\sigma[x \hookleftarrow v](y) = \begin{cases} v & \text{if } y = x \\ \sigma(y) & \text{otherwise} \end{cases}$$

and we naturally extend the notation to an arbitrary number of variables, *i.e.*, $\sigma[x_0 \hookleftarrow v_0, \dots, x_n \hookleftarrow v_n] = (\cdots(\sigma[x_0 \hookleftarrow v_0])\cdots)[x_n \hookleftarrow v_n]$. We also extend this notation to a function definition map ρ.

Finally, given a state $\pi = (\dot{\sigma}, \gamma, \rho)$ where $\dot{\sigma} = \sigma_0 \dots \sigma_n$, the *appending* of a new environment σ to $\dot{\sigma}$ is defined by $\pi \triangleleft \sigma = (\dot{\sigma} \triangleleft \sigma, \gamma, \rho) = (\sigma_0 \dots \sigma_n \sigma, \gamma, \rho)$, whereas the *dropping* of the last component of $\dot{\sigma}$ is denoted by $\pi_\downarrow = (\dot{\sigma}_\downarrow, \gamma, \rho) = (\sigma_0 \dots \sigma_{n-1}, \gamma, \rho)$ if $n > 0$. The *access* to the value of a variable x in π is defined by

$$\pi(x) = \begin{cases} \sigma_n(x) & \text{if } \sigma_n(x) \neq \bot \\ \gamma(x) & \text{otherwise} \end{cases}$$

This last definition actually formalizes the *shadowing* of global variables by local ones.

3) Operational Semantics: Given the above definitions, we provide the *small-step operational semantics* à la Plotkin [7]. In particular, we define the binary relation $\to$ over the set $\Pi \times \mathcal{T}$ accordingly to the inference rules provided in the next sections. Because of space limitations, we do not describe the semantics of the standard operations of the language (for which we redirect the reader to [8]), but we only focus on the key features of Chameleon.

Semantics of Function Calls: In order to compute the resulting value of an arbitrary function call $f(e_1, \dots, e_n)$ in a computational state $\pi = (\dot{\sigma}, \gamma, \rho)$, Chameleon implements a call-by-value strategy: Firstly, all actual parameters $e_0, \dots, e_n$ are evaluated to a ground value (rule FUNCALL). Then, if the function f is undefined in ρ, the undefined value is returned (rule FUNCALL-B1), otherwise a new environment in which the bindings between actual and formal parameters are defined is appended to $\dot{\sigma}$, and the computation continues from the function body (rules FUNCALL-B2 and FUNCALL-B3).

Semantics of Type Casting: The explicit type conversion $(t)\ e$ allows programmers to change the value of the expression e from its original type to the new type t. For each type t, we define a conversion function $\hookrightarrow_t$ that implements the type cast policy. More precisely, $\hookrightarrow_t : \mathbb{V} \to \mathbb{V}_t$ moves values from $\mathbb{V}$ to $\mathbb{V}_t = \{v \in \mathbb{V} \mid \tau(v) = t\}$, accordingly to the type of the input value, namely $\hookrightarrow_t (v) = \hookrightarrow_{t,\tau(v)} (v)$ where $\hookrightarrow_{t,\tau(v)} : \mathbb{V}_t \to \mathbb{V}_{\tau(v)}$. Given two types t and t', the definition of these functions is the standard conversion if t and t' are simple types, the identity function if $t = t'$, and otherwise $\hookrightarrow_{t,t'} (v)$ is inductively defined as follows:

$$\begin{cases} \hookrightarrow_{t,t'} (v) = \bot & \text{if } t \text{ or } t' \text{ is a simple type} \\ \hookrightarrow_{t,t'} (v) = \bot & \text{if } t, t' \notin \tau(\mathbb{L}) \text{ or } t, t' \notin \tau(\mathbb{D}) \\ \hookrightarrow_{t,t'} (v) = \bot & \text{if } |t| \neq |t'| \\ \hookrightarrow_{t,t'} ([v_1, \dots, v_n]) = [\hookrightarrow_{t'_1} (v_1), \dots, \hookrightarrow_{t'_n} (v_n)] \\ \quad \text{if } t' = [t'_0, \dots, t'_n] \\ \hookrightarrow_{t,t'} ([x_0 : v_0, \dots, x_n : v_n]) = \\ \quad [x_0 : \hookrightarrow_{t'_0} (v_1), \dots, x_n : \hookrightarrow_{t'_n} (v_n)] \\ \quad \text{if } t' \sim [x_0 : t'_0, \dots, x_n : t'_n] \end{cases}$$

For instance, concerning simple types, if v = "b4r" then $\hookrightarrow_{\texttt{str,int}} (v) = 4$, or if $v = \texttt{0}$, then $\hookrightarrow_{\texttt{int,bool}} (v) = \texttt{false}$, or if $v = \texttt{3.5}$, then $\hookrightarrow_{\texttt{int,str}} (v) =$ "3.5", etc. Given these premises, the rules CAST and CAST-B are now self-explanatory.

Reflection and Non-Determinism: The eval e statement enables the runtime execution of Chameleon code dynamically crafted by programs. Rule EVAL evaluates the expression e until a value v is obtained. If v = "P" is a string representing a valid Chameleon program, then $\hat{P}$ (namely, the unescaped version of P) is executed in the state π (thus, allowing side effects, see EVAL-B1). Otherwise, if v is not the representation of a valid program, $\bot$ is returned (EVAL-B2).

On the other hand, the input() expression allows *unbounded non-determinism* [9]. The implementation of the input() statement requires the user to supply an input (*i.e.*, a string) before continuing the computation. From the trace semantics point of view, any $s \in \mathbb{S}$ is a possible outcome of these statement, as modeled by the rule INPUT.

Operations and Type Coercion: Chameleon employs a neat type coercion system in order to let values to transparently

$$\textsc{ParExp}\ \frac{\langle \pi, e\rangle \to \langle \pi', e'\rangle}{\langle \pi, (e)\rangle \to \langle \pi', (e')\rangle} \qquad \textsc{ParExp-B}\ \frac{-}{\langle \pi, (v)\rangle \to \langle \pi, v\rangle}$$

$$\textsc{Id}\ \frac{-}{\langle \pi, x\rangle \to \langle \pi, \pi(x)\rangle}$$

$$\textsc{FunCall}\ \frac{\langle \pi, e_{i+1}\rangle \to \langle \pi', e'_{i+1}\rangle}{\langle \pi, f(v_1, \dots, v_i, e_{i+1}, \dots, e_n)\rangle \to \langle \pi', f(v_1, \dots, v_i, e'_{i+1}, \dots, e_n)\rangle}$$

$$\textsc{FunCall-B1}\ \frac{-}{\langle \pi, f(v_1, \dots, v_n)\rangle \to \langle \pi, \bot\rangle}\ \rho(f) = \bot$$

$$\textsc{FunCall-B2}\ \frac{-}{\langle \pi, f(v_1, \dots, v_n)\rangle \to \langle \pi \triangleleft \{ x_1 \hookleftarrow v_1, \dots, x_m \hookleftarrow v_m \}, c\rangle}\ \rho(f) = ((x_1, \dots, x_m), c) \wedge n \geq m$$

$$\textsc{FunCall-B3}\ \frac{-}{\langle \pi, f(v_1, \dots, v_n)\rangle \to \langle \pi \triangleleft \{ x_1 \hookleftarrow v_1, \dots, x_n \hookleftarrow v_n \}, c\rangle}\ \rho(f) = ((x_1, \dots, x_m), c) \wedge n < m$$

$$\textsc{Cast}\ \frac{\langle \pi, e\rangle \to \langle \pi', e'\rangle}{\langle \pi, (t)\ e\rangle \to \langle \pi', (t)\ e'\rangle} \qquad \textsc{Cast-B}\ \frac{-}{\langle \pi, (t)\ v\rangle \to \langle \pi, \hookrightarrow_t (v)\rangle}$$

$$\textsc{Eval}\ \frac{\langle \pi, e\rangle \to \langle \pi', e'\rangle}{\langle \pi, \mathtt{eval}\ e\rangle \to \langle \pi', \mathtt{eval}\ e'\rangle} \qquad \textsc{Eval-B1}\ \frac{-}{\langle \pi, \mathtt{eval}\ v\rangle \to \langle \pi, \hat{P}\rangle}\ \exists \hat{P} \in \langle prog\rangle \,.\, v = \text{“}P\text{”}$$

$$\textsc{Eval-B2}\ \frac{-}{\langle \pi, \mathtt{eval}\ v\rangle \to \langle \pi, \bot\rangle}\ \nexists \hat{P} \in \langle prog\rangle \,.\, v = \text{“}P\text{”}$$

$$\textsc{Input}\ \frac{-}{\langle \pi, \mathtt{input()}\rangle \to \langle \pi, s\rangle}\ \forall s \in \mathbb{S}$$

Figure 2. Small-step semantics of Chameleon expressions.

flow from one type to another when needed. Suppose that $\otimes \in \langle bop\rangle$ is defined for integers and rationals and let us denote by $\otimes_{\mathtt{int}} \colon \mathbb{V}^2_{\mathtt{int}} \to \mathbb{V}_{\mathtt{int}}$ and $\otimes_{\mathtt{rat}} \colon \mathbb{V}^2_{\mathtt{rat}} \to \mathbb{V}_{\mathtt{rat}}$ the typed versions of $\otimes$. Consider the expression $v \otimes v'$ for two arbitrary ground values: The goal is to get a value $v'' = v \otimes v'$ in a way that depends only on the set of types on which $\otimes$ is defined. For instance, if $\otimes = \star$, we want to provide a meaning to expressions like `(true * "a")`, `(5 * false)`, etc. Note that computing v'' is not a trivial task, especially when seeking a general method.

The strategy implemented in the Chameleon interpreter is based on the previously defined partial order $\preccurlyeq$ on types. The algorithm for the computation of v'' is described as follows:

1) We compute the set of types on which $\otimes$ is defined, namely $\mathrm{dom}(\otimes) = \{ \bot \} \cup \{ \mathtt{int}, \mathtt{rat} \} \cup \tau(\mathbb{L}) \cup \tau(\mathbb{D})$. By this definition, every operator is defined on the undefined type in a vacuous manner, and inductively on compound types. More precisely, this means that $\bot \otimes v = v \otimes \bot = \bot$, and if $v_0, v'_0 \dots, v_n, v'_n$ is a sequence of values, then $[v_0, \dots, v_n] \otimes [v'_0, \dots, v'_n] = [v_0 \otimes v'_0, \dots, v_n \otimes v'_n]$ and similarly for dictionary values;
2) We refine $\mathrm{dom}(\otimes)$ in order to get all the types greater than $\tau(v)$ or $\tau(v')$, namely $\mathrm{dom}_\uparrow(\otimes) = \{ t \in \mathrm{dom}(\otimes) \mid t \geq \tau(v) \vee t \geq \tau(v') \}$, and the types lower than $\tau(v)$ or $\tau(v')$, namely $\mathrm{dom}_\downarrow(\otimes) = \{ t \in \mathrm{dom}(\otimes) \mid t \leq \tau(v) \vee t \leq \tau(v') \}$;
3) We compute the least upper bound between (i) the greatest lower bound of $\mathrm{dom}_\uparrow(\otimes)$ and (ii) the least upper bound of $\mathrm{dom}_\downarrow(\otimes)$, namely $t = \bigvee\{ \wedge \mathrm{dom}_\uparrow(\otimes), \vee \mathrm{dom}_\downarrow(\otimes) \}$;
4) The result of the computation is defined as $v'' = v \otimes_t v'$.

The rules for computing the result of a binary operation are now trivial. Firstly, we evaluate left-to-right the expressions in the operation until values are obtained:

$$\textsc{Exp-L}\ \frac{\langle \pi, e_1\rangle \to \langle \pi', e'_1\rangle}{\langle \pi, e_1 \otimes e_2\rangle \to \langle \pi', e'_1 \otimes e_2\rangle} \qquad \textsc{Exp-R}\ \frac{\langle \pi, e_2\rangle \to \langle \pi', e'_2\rangle}{\langle \pi, v \otimes e_2\rangle \to \langle \pi', v \otimes e'_2\rangle}$$

Then, we compute the result applying the algorithm described above:

$$\textsc{Exp-B}\ \frac{-}{\langle \pi, v \otimes v'\rangle \to \langle \pi', v''\rangle}$$

where $v'' = v \otimes_t v'$ and $t = \bigvee\{ \wedge \mathrm{dom}_\uparrow(\otimes), \vee \mathrm{dom}_\downarrow(\otimes) \}$.

Commands and Return Statement: Since most of Chameleon commands are common to the majority of the imperative languages, we only discuss here the rule of the return statement, and we redirect the reader to [8] for a detailed explanation of the other commands.

When a `return` e statement is met, the expression e is evaluated in order to obtain a value v:

$$\text{RET}\ \frac{\langle \pi, e\rangle \rightarrow \langle \pi', e'\rangle}{\langle \pi, \texttt{return}\ e\rangle \rightarrow \langle \pi', \texttt{return}\ e'\rangle}$$

Then, the following rule returns the value v and restores the bindings existing previously of the function call:

$$\text{RET-B}\ \frac{-}{\langle \pi, \texttt{return}\ v\rangle \rightarrow \langle \pi_{\downarrow}, v\rangle}$$

III. Conclusion

In this paper, we have presented Chameleon, a minimal language capturing the main features of dynamic programming languages. In particular, it is an imperative non-deterministic language with functions/procedures and built-in inductive data-structures, such as finite lists and finite dictionaries. Concerning the dynamic features, Chameleon is not statically typed, with a mechanism for type coercion. It supports (limited) reflection, implemented by means of an eval-like construct, and expressions can have side-effects.

The aim of Chameleon is to provide a common ground for static analyses developers, in order to easily define and test their control mechanisms. To build an analyzer for a real-world programming language is a complex engineering task. Chameleon abstracts all the technical details characterizing each language, allowing developers to focus on the analysis of dynamic features only and, hence, to define new analyses in a faster and simpler way. Furthermore, comparing similar control mechanisms, but built for different languages, is tricky. With Chameleon, is it possible to solve also this issue, since the analyses share the same underling language.

As a final remark, the interested reader can find the implementation of Chameleon at the following link: `https://github.com/samueleburo93/chameleon`.

References

[1] G. A. Kildall, "A unified approach to global program optimization," in Proceedings of the 1st Annual ACM SIGACT-SIGPLAN Symposium on Principles of Programming Languages, ser. POPL '73, 1973, pp. 194–206.

[2] P. Cousot and R. Cousot, "Abstract interpretation: A unified lattice model for static analysis of programs by construction or approximation of fix-points," in Proceedings of the 4th ACM SIGACT-SIGPLAN Symposium on Principles of Programming Languages, ser. POPL '77, 1977, pp. 238–252.

[3] E. M. Clarke, E. A. Emerson, and A. P. Sistla, "Automatic verification of finite-state concurrent systems using temporal logic specifications," ACM Trans. Program. Lang. Syst., vol. 8, 1986, pp. 244–263.

[4] V. Arceri and S. Maffeis, "Abstract domains for type juggling," Electr. Notes Theor. Comput. Sci., vol. 331, 2017, pp. 41–55.

[5] S. Buro and I. Mastroeni, "Abstract code injection - A semantic approach based on abstract non-interference," in Proceedings of the 19th International Conference on Verification, Model Checking, and Abstract Interpretation, ser. VMCAI '18, 2018, pp. 116–137.

[6] I. Mastroeni and M. Pasqua, "Statically analyzing information flows: An abstract interpretation-based hyperanalysis for non-interference," in Proceedings of the 34th ACM/SIGAPP Symposium on Applied Computing, ser. SAC '19, 2019, pp. 2215–2223.

[7] G. D. Plotkin, "A structural approach to operational semantics," Journal of Logic and Algebraic Programming, vol. 60-61, 2004, pp. 17–139. [Online]. Available: http://dx.doi.org/10.1016/j.jlap.2004.05.001

[8] M. Hennessy, The Semantics of Programming Languages: An Elementary Introduction Using Structural Operational Semantics. New York, NY, USA: John Wiley & Sons, Inc., 1990.

[9] G. D. Plotkin, "A powerdomain for countable non-determinism," in Proceedings of the 9th International Colloquium on Automata, Languages and Programming, 1982, pp. 418–428.

A Taint Analyzer for COBOL Programs

Alberto Lovato
University of Verona
Verona, Italy
Email: alberto.lovato@univr.it

Roberto Giacobazzi
University of Verona
Verona, Italy
Email: roberto.giacobazzi@univr.it

Isabella Mastroeni
University of Verona
Verona, Italy
Email: isabella.mastroeni@univr.it

***Abstract*—The potential damage injection attacks or information leakage can inflict to an organization is huge. It is therefore important to recognize vulnerabilities in software that can make these attacks possible. We are implementing a static analysis that tracks propagation of tainted values through a COBOL-85 program. This analysis is part of an already developed static analyzer performing many syntactic checks and a semantic interval analysis. It can be used to find untrusted values ending in dangerous places, for example executed as database queries, or to verify that sensitive information coming from a database is not displayed to the user.**

Keywords–Taint analysis; Injection attacks; Information leakage; COBOL.

I. Introduction

COBOL is a programming language for business use. It was designed in 1959, and is still employed in many organizations. The existing codebase is huge, and experienced COBOL programmers are aiming for retirement. Many organizations have migration plans, but a substantial part of COBOL code is not going to be dismantled in the foreseeable future. Being used for security critical tasks, e.g., transactions between bank accounts, it is important to verify that COBOL programs have as few vulnerabilities as possible. COBOL-85 programs are structured into *divisions*. In particular, the *data division* contains variable declarations, and the *procedure division* contains executable code. It is imperative, structured code, with no object-orientation.

This paper describes a prototype of a static analyzer for tracking of values that we consider *tainted*—e.g., coming from the user (untrusted), or from a database (sensitive)—in COBOL-85 code. This is done by first translating the program into an internal, simpler language, only considering modification of strings, and then by defining a *transfer function* propagating tainted values. The transfer function is applied by an *interpreter* to each statement of the intermediate program, to update the set of tainted variables at that program point.

Injections are the top vulnerabilities found in web applications [1], and although COBOL is generally not used in front end development, it can still be used in the back end part of the application. It is therefore desirable to be able to find injection vulnerabilities in COBOL code.

Injection detection in other languages is well studied, for example for the Java language [2], [3], JavaScript [4], Android [5], scripting languages, e.g., Python [6], and even web frameworks [7]. However, to our knowledge, taint analysis in COBOL is not considered in the academic community.

The paper is structured as follows. Section II describes the ARCTIC analyzer, that contains the code for the taint analysis that is explained in the paper. In Section III, the analysis is described in detail. In Section IV, the analysis of a small COBOL program is executed. Section V concludes the paper.

II. The ARCTIC Analyzer

The analysis code is part of ARCTIC, a general static analyzer for COBOL-85 programs.

ARCTIC currently performs a lot of syntactic analyses, along with a semantic analysis for the computation of variable intervals. More precise numerical analyses are in development. Interval analysis also is executed on a simpler internal language, this time only considering modification to numerical variables.

ARCTIC is written in Java, has command-line and remote interfaces, and can be run by a *SonarQube* [8] plug-in. SonarQube is a platform used in many organizations to run analyzers and tools for code quality management of software projects. A *scanner* module is responsible for running analyses on code and sending the result to the *server* module. A user can then connect to the server with a browser to look at nicely formatted statistics and issues. The SonarQube plug-in of ARCTIC sends analysis *rules* selected by the SonarQube user and the paths of files of the project to the ARCTIC server, which analyzes them and sends issues back to the plug-in.

The interaction between ARCTIC and SonarQube is shown in Figure 1.

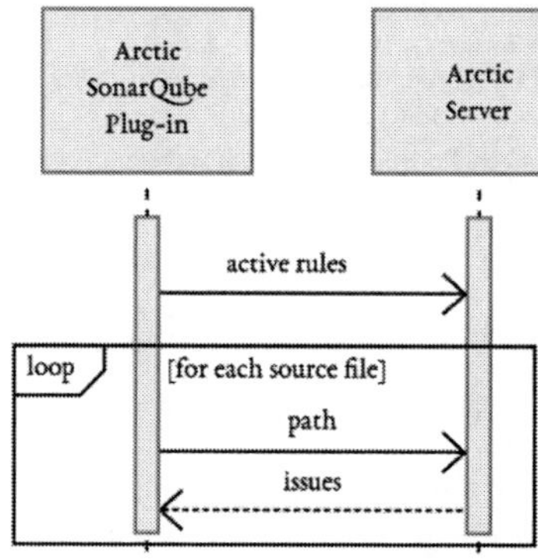

Figure 1. Interaction between the ARCTIC server and the *SonarQube* plug-in.

Issues are then available to be displayed in the SonarQube web interface. In Figure 2, there is an example result of taint analysis performed by ARCTIC, as seen by a user connecting to the SonarQube server with a browser. Issues are shown below the line to which they belong, after the user clicks on issue markers on the left. In this example, the analysis output is a set of variables that are tainted before reaching every program point, and so are the issues.

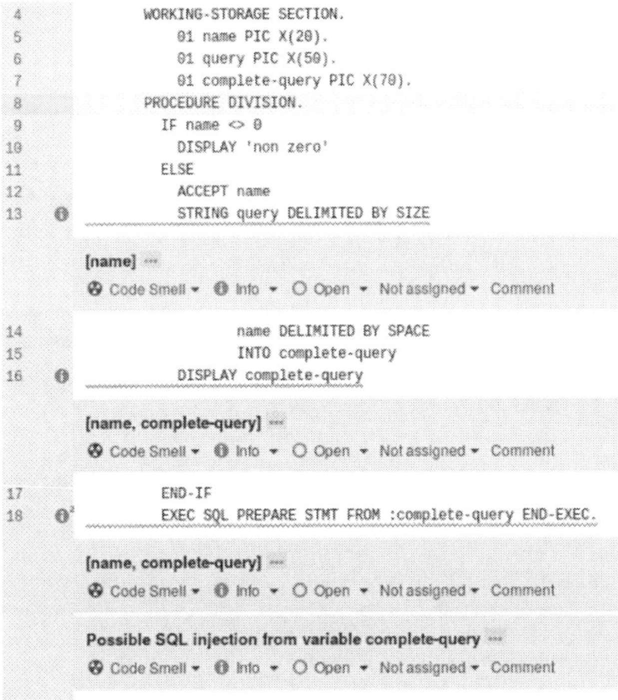

Figure 2. Taint analysis output displayed in the *SonarQube* web interface.

SonarQube rules represent some kinds of condition that users want to check. Rules may be activated in user defined *quality profiles*. Figure 3 is a screenshot of some rules defined in the ARCTIC SonarQube plug-in.

SonarQube itself contains a module for analysis of COBOL programs [9] in its Enterprise Edition, but at present it does not perform taint nor interval analysis.

ARCTIC uses a parser for COBOL-85 code that is a fork of *proleap-cobol-parser* [10], supporting ANSI 85, IBM OS/VS and MicroFocus dialects. The Abstract Syntax Tree (AST) produced by the parser contains representations of COBOL components, such as divisions, statements and declarations in a hierarchical way. Nodes of the AST can be accessed by using the *visitor* pattern, that allows client programmers to act on elements of a certain type by simply overriding a method in a class. Syntactic checks can be performed right after parsing, to detect situations like obsolete or insecure statements, bad coding practices, and type errors. Some other analyses verify the correctness of SQL code embedded into COBOL programs. This SQL code is extracted by the COBOL parser from `EXEC SQL` statements, and then parsed and analyzed with the aid of an external library, *JSqlParser* [11].

III. TAINT ANALYSIS

The analyzer works by interpreting the code, in order to compute a representation of the state where, at each program point, it is clear which variables are tainted. It considers a version of the program containing only relevant information, such as data about text variables and statements manipulating or using them. This simplifies the analysis a lot, as COBOL code is very verbose, and many statements are redundant for the analysis. The translation process is explained in Section III-A. The state in our case is simply the set of tainted variables at each program point. The interpreter executes each statement of the intermediate language by giving to it as input state the output state of the previous one, as shown in Figure 4.

The initial state is in general empty, as no variable is tainted at start. However, procedure divisions in COBOL may have *parameters*, since they can be called as subprograms by other programs. We do not analyze flows between programs yet, but the user can specify a flag, in order to consider parameters of procedure divisions as tainted. For each statement, the analysis tracks the current tainted variables, and if they flow into a sink, an issue is reported. An example is shown in Table I.

TABLE I. EXAMPLE PROGRAM ANALYSIS.

State before	Statement
$\emptyset$	**DISPLAY** x
$\emptyset$	**ACCEPT** x
$\{x\}$	**STRING** '**Input:** ' x **DELIMITED BY SPACE INTO** y
$\{x, y\}$	...
$\{x, y\}$	$sink(y) \leftarrow$ report issue

Here, the second statement adds the variable x to the set, since its content is coming from the user. The following statement transfers taintedness to variable y. Lastly, the tainted value reaches a sink, and the analyzer reports an issue.

A. Translation

If we are interested in detecting injection of untrusted data, for example in a database query, we have to look for text variables, as numerical variables cannot be used to perform an injection attack.

ACCEPT. The means by which a user could directly insert a value into a COBOL-85 standard program is the **ACCEPT** statement, that reads input from the console, and is as such considered a source of untrusted data. It is translated into ***ACCEPT*** x, where x is the variable receiving the data, unless the statement accepts data from the system date; in that case it is translated into ***SKIP***, since the date is not an untrusted input.

STRING. The **STRING** statement concatenates several strings into one. It is translated into the intermediate statement ***STRING*** $x_1, \ldots, x_n$ ***INTO*** y.

MOVE. The **MOVE** statement moves the value of a variable into another variable. It is translated into ***MOVE*** x ***TO*** y.

Paragraphs. COBOL code is organized in paragraphs, labeled blocks of code. Procedure calls are implemented in COBOL by using the **PERFORM** statement, followed by the names of the blocks to execute, which form the body of the procedure. Considering for example a code subdivided in three paragraphs like this

```
PAR1.
  ACCEPT name
  DISPLAY name.
  ...
PAR2.
```

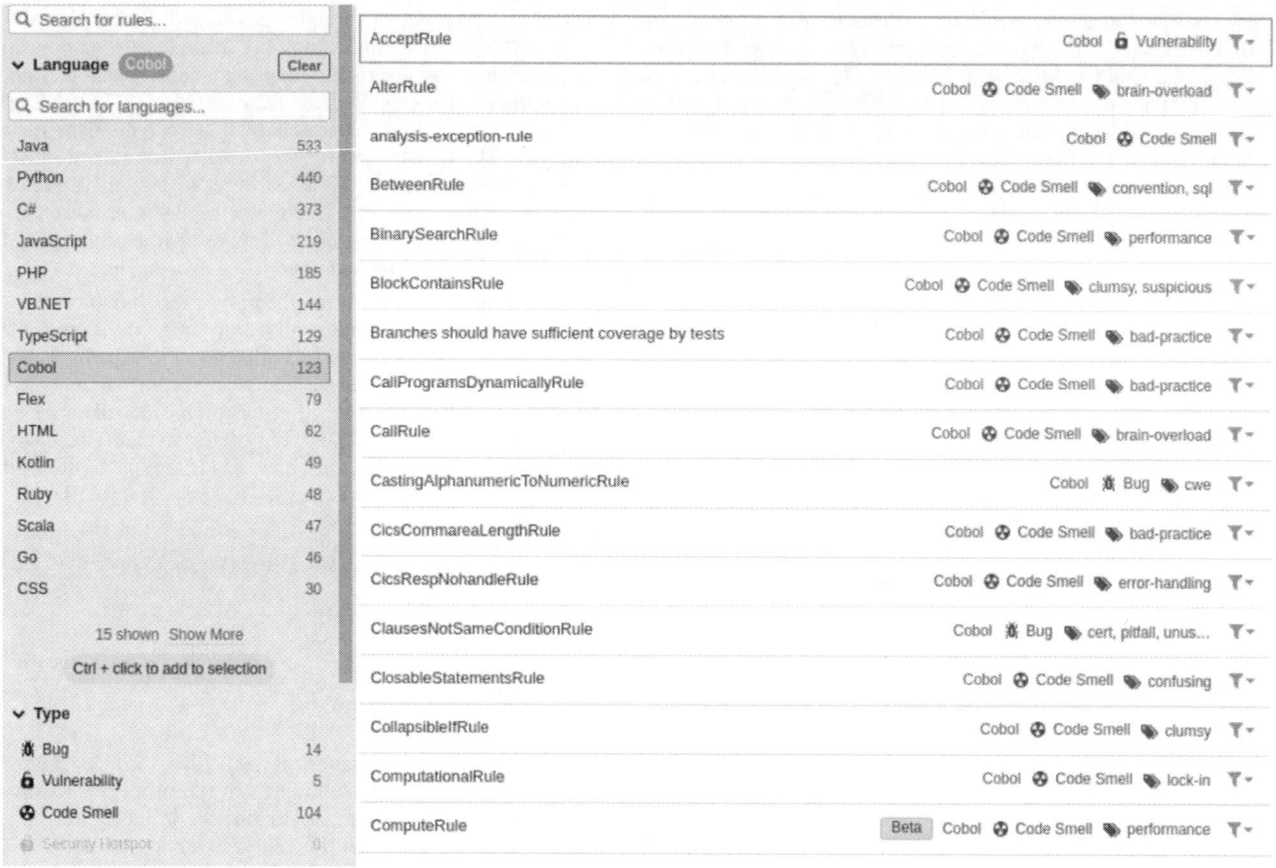

Figure 3. ARCTIC rule list in the SonarQube plug-in

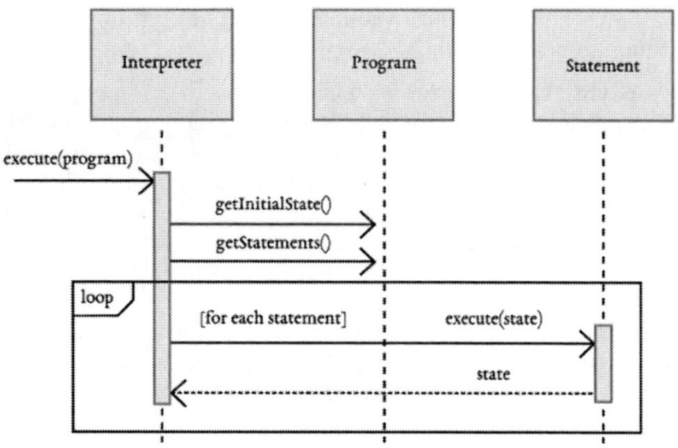

Figure 4. Execution of the program by the interpreter.

```
    ...
PAR3.
    ...
```

a single block would be called with **PERFORM** PAR1, whereas a sequence of blocks would be called with something like **PERFORM** PAR1 **THRU** PAR3. Procedure calling statements like those above are translated into *EXECUTEBLOCKS first [last]*. **PERFORM** can also describe loops, with the clause **UNTIL**, that repeats the body of the statement until a certain condition becomes true, or with the clause **TIMES**, that repeats the body of the statement a specified number of times. Taintedness does not change in loops, so these statements are translated like any other kind of **PERFORM**.

Injection. We are also interested in statements that may cause the unintended execution of code. For SQL injection, the statement `EXEC SQL PREPARE STMT FROM :DYNSTMT END-EXEC` executes a possibly dynamically created query stored in `DYNSTMT`. It is translated into *EXECSQLPREPARE DYNSTMT*. These statements, where flow of tainted information can cause unintended interaction with other parts of the system, are called *sinks*. We also denote the previous statement by $sink$(DYNSTMT).

Control flow statements. **IF** statements execute a branch or another according to the valuation of a condition. The corresponding intermediate statement is *IF condition THEN* B_1 *ELSE* B_2, where B_1 and B_2 are blocks of intermediate statements.

Other statements. Statements that do not deal with string manipulation are translated into the intermediate statement *SKIP*, that is ignored by the analysis.

Intermediate statements store information about the original COBOL statement, such as the line number, in order to map issues back to the original position in the source code. They also store the state before their execution, so that it is readily available to be displayed at the right program point.

B. Transfer Function

Let $\mathbf{T}$ be the set of all sets of tainted variables. We define a transfer function $f : \mathbf{T} \to \mathbf{T}$ that specifies which variables are tainted after the execution of each statement, given the input state $T \in \mathbf{T}$. The interpreter implements this transfer function in the `execute` method of the class corresponding to each statement type, to produce a set of tainted variables for every program point.

ACCEPT x**.** This statement gets an input string directly from the user. This is a potential source of untrusted data, and so we mark the receiving variable as tainted.

$$f_{ACCEPT}(T) = T \cup \{x\} \tag{1}$$

STRING $x_1, \ldots, x_n$ **INTO** y**.** String values are concatenated with the **STRING** statement, that as such transfers the taintedness properties from source variables to the receiving variable. If at least one of the variables containing the strings that are being concatenated is tainted, then we mark the receiving variable as tainted.

$$f_{STRING}(T) = \begin{cases} T \cup \{y\} & \text{if } \exists x \in \{x_1, \ldots, x_n\}.x \in T \\ T & \text{otherwise} \end{cases} \tag{2}$$

MOVE x **TO** y**.** **MOVE** makes the receiving variable tainted if and only if the source variable is tainted.

$$f_{MOVE}(T) = \begin{cases} T \cup \{y\} & \text{if } x \in T \\ T & \text{otherwise} \end{cases} \tag{3}$$

Paragraphs. Each paragraph is a list of statements, e.g., $P1 = S_1 \ldots S_n$; the transfer function of a paragraph is the composition of the transfer functions of the statements.

$$f_{P1}(T) = f_{S_n}(\ldots(f_{S_1}(T))\ldots) \tag{4}$$

EXECUTEBLOCKS $first$ **[**$last$**].** For every COBOL program, we build a list of blocks corresponding to its paragraphs, for example `P1, P2, P3`. When we then execute a block with the intermediate statement EXECUTEBLOCKS P1, its transfer function is that of the executed block.

$$f_{EB}(T) = f_{P1}(T) \tag{5}$$

The transfer function of the execution of several blocks, e.g., EXECUTEBLOCKS P1 P3, is the composition of the functions of the executed blocks.

$$f_{EB}(T) = f_{P3}(f_{P2}(f_{P1}(T))) \tag{6}$$

IF $condition$ **THEN** B_1 **ELSE** B_2**.** We conservatively keep taintedness information of both branches of a conditional statement, and so the transfer function is the union of the two functions.

$$f_{IF}(T) = f_{B_1}(T) \cup f_{B_2}(T) \tag{7}$$

SKIP. This statement does nothing regarding the modification of taintedness of variables, and so its transfer function is the identity function.

$$f_{SKIP}(T) = T \tag{8}$$

Sinks do not modify taintedness, and thus they have an identity transfer function. Table II sums up translation and transfer function result for every intermediate statement.

C. Implementation

Figure 5 shows the transformation of a COBOL program. Variables containing text are extracted in a list, whereas COBOL statements are translated into intermediate language. A list of the paragraphs found in the program is kept in memory to allow the interpreter to execute EXECUTEBLOCKS statements.

Figure 6 outlines the execution of the intermediate program. The interpreter executes the transfer function of every statement, and the produced state is retained in the executed program, associated to the next statement.

IV. EXAMPLE

In this section, we reconsider the example of Figure 2, and show how it is transformed and executed.

```
1         IDENTIFICATION DIVISION.
2         PROGRAM-ID. example.
3         DATA DIVISION.
4         WORKING-STORAGE SECTION.
5             01 name PIC X(20).
6             01 query PIC X(50).
7             01 complete-query PIC
                 X(70).
8         PROCEDURE DIVISION.
9          PAR1.
10          IF name <> 0
11            DISPLAY 'non zero'
12          ELSE
13            ACCEPT name
14            STRING query DELIMITED BY
                SIZE
15                  name DELIMITED BY
                      SPACE
16                  INTO complete-query
17            DISPLAY complete-query
18          END-IF
19         PAR2.
20          EXEC SQL PREPARE STMT FROM
              :complete-query END-EXEC.
```

Three alphanumerical variables are declared at lines 5-7, so the variable list `name, query, complete-query` is produced by the `VariableExtractor`. The paragraph list `PAR1, PAR2` is saved in the intermediate program. The `IF` statement at lines 10-18 is translated as

```
IF condition
  SKIP
ELSE
  ACCEPT name
  STRING query, name INTO complete-query
  SKIP
```

TABLE II. TRANSFER FUNCTION f.

COBOL	Intermediate	$f(T)$
ACCEPT <identifier>	ACCEPT x	$T \cup \{x\}$
STRING ... **INTO** ...	STRING $x_1, \ldots, x_n$ INTO y	$\begin{cases} T \cup \{y\} & \text{if } \exists x \in \{x_1, \ldots, x_n\}. x \in T \\ T & \text{otherwise} \end{cases}$
MOVE ... **TO** ...	MOVE x TO y	$\begin{cases} T \cup \{y\} & \text{if } x \in T \\ T & \text{otherwise} \end{cases}$
P1. <statements>	P1 = $S_1 \ldots S_n$	$f_{S_n}(\ldots(f_{S_1}(T))\ldots)$
PERFORM P1	EXECUTEBLOCKS P1	$f_{P1}(T)$
PERFORM P1 **THRU** P3	EXECUTEBLOCKS P1 P3	$f_{P3}(f_{P2}(f_{P1}(T)))$
control flow	IF condition THEN B_1 ELSE B_2	$f_{B_1}(T) \cup f_{B_2}(T)$
sinks	e.g., EXECSQLPREPARE source	T
other statements	SKIP	T

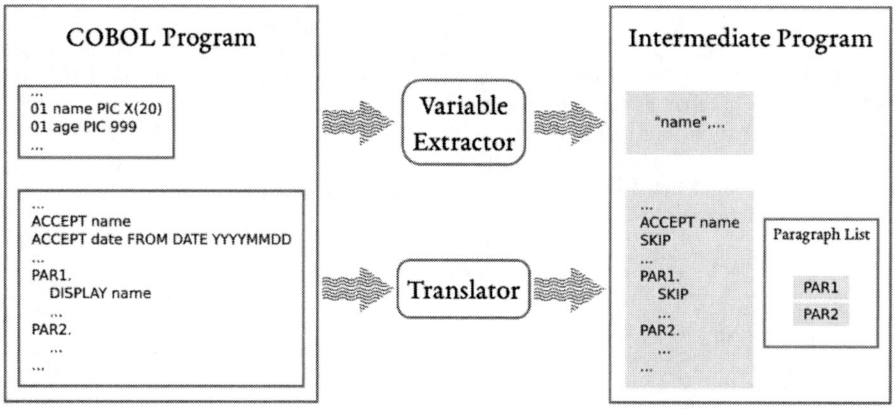

Figure 5. Transformation of a COBOL program into the intermediate representation.

Figure 6. Execution of the intermediate program by the interpreter.

whereas the statement at line 20 is translated as

```
EXECSQLPREPARE complete-query
```

Then, each statement is executed by applying the logic defined in Section III-B. For example, the transfer function of the IF statement is defined as

$$\begin{aligned} f_{IF}(T) &= f_{SKIP}(T) \cup f_{SKIP}(f_{STRING}(f_{ACCEPT}(T))) \\ &\overset{(8)}{=} T \cup f_{STRING}(f_{ACCEPT}(T)) \\ &\overset{(1)}{=} T \cup f_{STRING}(T \cup \{\texttt{name}\}) \\ &\overset{(2)}{=} T \cup T \cup \{\texttt{name}, \texttt{complete-query}\}) \\ &= T \cup \{\texttt{name}, \texttt{complete-query}\} \end{aligned}$$

Before executing the `IF` statement, the set T is empty, since none of the declared variables are tainted at that point. The final set is thus $\{\texttt{name}, \texttt{complete-query}\}$.

V. CONCLUSION

The prototype we developed is able to track propagation of tainted values in COBOL-85 programs. We are not aware of any other taint analyzer for COBOL code. At the moment, the analyzer only checks for SQL-injection, but, as future work, we could also consider other kinds of injection, or the other way round, the leaking of sensitive values. Information from a database, e.g., a credit card number, may be displayed to the user if a variable containing it is used as argument of the COBOL statement **DISPLAY**. This kind of analysis would require considering **DISPLAY** statements and analogous ones (e.g., GUI output statements) as sinks, while sources of tainted information would be statements reading from the database into host variables. Also, other versions of COBOL may allow users to inject values via other means, e.g., a graphical user interface, and not only via the **ACCEPT** statement, so we may extend the analysis to include this possibility.

REFERENCES

[1] "Owasp Top 10 Project," 2019, URL: https://www.owasp.org/index.php/Category:OWASP_Top_Ten_Project [retrieved: 2019-10-27].

[2] F. Spoto, E. Burato, M. D. Ernst, P. Ferrara, A. Lovato, D. Macedonio, and C. Spiridon, "Static Identification of Injection Attacks in Java," ACM Trans. Program. Lang. Syst., vol. 41, no. 3, 2019, pp. 18:1–18:58.

[3] O. Tripp, M. Pistoia, S. J. Fink, M. Sridharan, and O. Weisman, "TAJ: effective taint analysis of web applications," in Proceedings of the 2009 ACM SIGPLAN Conference on Programming Language Design and Implementation, PLDI 2009, Dublin, Ireland, June 15-21, 2009, 2009, pp. 87–97.

[4] S. Guarnieri, M. Pistoia, O. Tripp, J. Dolby, S. Teilhet, and R. Berg, "Saving the World Wide Web from Vulnerable JavaScript," in Proceedings of the 2011 International Symposium on Software Testing and Analysis, ser. ISSTA '11. New York, NY, USA: ACM, 2011, pp. 177–187.

[5] S. Arzt, S. Rasthofer, C. Fritz, E. Bodden, A. Bartel, J. Klein, Y. Le Traon, D. Octeau, and P. McDaniel, "FlowDroid: Precise Context, Flow, Field, Object-sensitive and Lifecycle-aware Taint Analysis for Android Apps," in Proceedings of the 35th ACM SIGPLAN Conference on Programming Language Design and Implementation, ser. PLDI '14. New York, NY, USA: ACM, 2014, pp. 259–269.

[6] S. Liang and M. Might, "Hash-flow Taint Analysis of Higher-order Programs," in Proceedings of the 7th Workshop on Programming Languages and Analysis for Security, ser. PLAS '12. New York, NY, USA: ACM, 2012, pp. 8:1–8:12.

[7] M. Sridharan, S. Artzi, M. Pistoia, S. Guarnieri, O. Tripp, and R. Berg, "F4F: Taint Analysis of Framework-based Web Applications," in Proceedings of the 2011 ACM International Conference on Object Oriented Programming Systems Languages and Applications, ser. OOPSLA '11. New York, NY, USA: ACM, 2011, pp. 1053–1068.

[8] "SonarQube platform," 2019, URL: https://www.sonarqube.org [retrieved: 2019-10-27].

[9] "SonarCOBOL," 2019, URL: https://www.sonarsource.com/products/codeanalyzers/sonarcobol.html [retrieved: 2019-10-27].

[10] "Proleap Cobol Parser," 2019, URL: https://github.com/uwol/proleap-cobol-parser [retrieved: 2019-10-27].

[11] "Java SQL Parser," 2019, URL: https://github.com/JSQLParser/JSqlParser [retrieved: 2019-10-27].

How to Overcome Test Smells in an Automation Environment

Mesut Durukal
IOT Division
Siemens AS
Istanbul, Turkey
e-mail: mesut.durukal@siemens.com

Abstract—**This paper presents the most common test smells and their prevention methods in a test automation framework. In this scope, the necessity for test automation is discussed and the most probable test smells in a test automation framework are discussed. Possible solution methods to handle test smells are presented and their advantages are evaluated as per the obtained results. Presented methods are also applied in the test activities of a big project, which is a cloud-based open IoT operating system and consists of microservices.**

Keywords-cloud services; asynchronous microservices; test automation; test smells; robustness.

I. Introduction

It is a well-known fact that neglecting testing activities in projects can cause major cost impacts in the later stages of the product life cycle. To illustrate the prominence of testing, the leaning tower of Pisa is a stunning example for costs of fix after release. The project lasted for 10 years and its total cost was over €30 million [1]. Another example to support this is the annual cost of manual maintenance and evolution of test scripts in Accenture, which was estimated to be between $50-$120 million [2].

All levels of testing activities have to be incorporated into projects on time to avoid such situations. For the products/systems in which multiple units/subsystems are integrated, each unit or subsystem is tested individually. Nevertheless, the integrated product/system must still be verified, which indicates the necessity of end-to-end testing. The quality of the product is fully ensured by testing at all levels [3].

Once the importance of testing is accepted, the next concern would possibly be the testing approach. Necessity for test automation arises due to several reasons. Even though the demands are growing in projects since more requirements and features are added day by day, timelines tend to get shorter, and this increases the pressure on every stakeholder. Each activity in a project has to be managed more efficiently in terms of time and effort for this reason. Additionally, in a continuous integration and delivery environment, bugs possibly exist in each deployment, and hence the need of continuous testing is evident.

Continuous testing activities would be much more difficult to manage without test automation. Tests are automated and scheduled executions are planned and triggered automatically over pipelines to reduce manual effort and testing duration.

Although there is no doubt about the need of test automation, it has several challenges. One of the most encountered difficulty is the inconsistent results, especially in the asynchronous services. Therefore, robustness is very crucial for testers to avoid additional analysis effort. Test smell is the main cause of lack of robustness in test results. Proposed solutions in this paper provide an insight to cope with test smells and ensure robustness.

To sum up, testing is a must for quality of our products and hence the prevention of unexpected costs. Thanks to test automation, it is possible to perform testing activities, continuously. On the other hand, automation has some challenges since there is a risk for smells in test code. Test smells cause extra effort and cost. Main objectives of this paper are:

- To present the most common smells,
- To present a set of mitigating actions for those smells within the scope of automated testing,
- To provide empirical information supporting actions.

For this purpose, system under test is presented in Section II and Section III describes test smells. Section IV explains the solutions, where the results are discussed in Section V. Finally, summary of the work is addressed in Section VI.

II. System Under Test

The system under test has been developed by more than 600 people in 10 countries. A new version is released every two weeks. Acceptance tests are performed for each release and regression tests are performed after every deployment, which is approximately every 4 hours.

The architecture is built on microservices approach, which makes use of a granular structure. In this way, services collaborate and build the whole product. A representation of microservices architecture is shown in Figure 1.

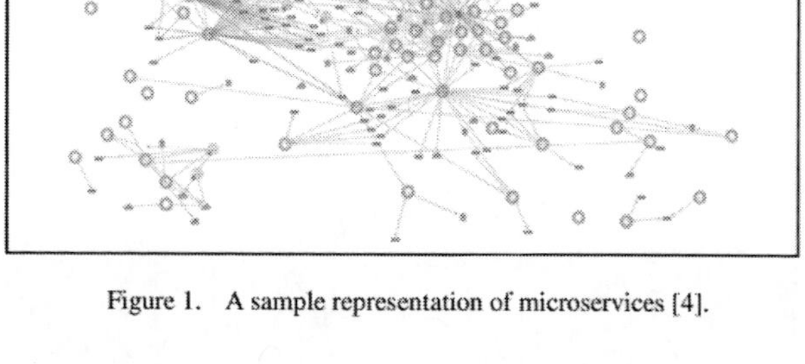

Figure 1. A sample representation of microservices [4].

Despite all the advantages [5], there are drawbacks as well, especially for asynchronous systems. In those systems, user requests are responded by the relevant unit without waiting for the response of the successive units. For each request, a transaction is created, which leads additional requests to other microservices. Even if the first steps of the transaction succeed, a failure in the following steps is possible. Unpredictable failures and processing time are underlying causes for test smells in such architectures.

III. Test Smells

Test smells are observed during the test cycles and the solutions are applied on a cloud-based open IoT operating system in this study. Testing activities are performed from unit level to end-to-end level.

Counter-actions against automation difficulties for test improvement are explained in Section IV. Before that, test smells are defined formally in this section in order to construct a framework for the proposals. Test smells are defined as indicators, observed during testing cycles, for potential problems [6]. In other words, they are regarded as signals for the poorly designed tests [7].

A good starting point to emphasize the importance of test smells is to explain their consequences if they are not fixed. Table I shows all possible test results, where the highlighted cells are two problematic groups. When a test does not catch a failure, this corresponds to the Silent Horror [8]. On the other hand, the situation, where a test result shows a failure even though the feature under test is developed as expected, indicates a False Alarm.

TABLE I. Test Results Classification [3]

		Correct Result	
		Pass	*Fail*
Execution Result	*Pass*	No Problem	Silent Horror
	Fail	False Alarm	Real Bugs

Silent Horrors cause extra costs in later stages of product life cycle, since the cost of fixing a bug after the release of the product considerably increases. According to [9], in such a situation the cost of bug fixing is nine times higher. That's to say, a test smell, which is a potential cause for such a problematic result, means additional cost in the product budget.

Similarly, false alarms cause extra costs as well, since the reported false alarms require an evaluation. To illustrate how crucial they can be, crash of Helios Airways Flight 522 in August 2005 can be examined. It is the most fatal flight accident to date in which 121 passengers and crew were killed when a Boeing 737-31S crashed into a mountain in the north of Athens [10]. After the accident investigation, it was concluded that the pilots neglected the cockpit pressure failure alarms due to lots of false alarms. The existence of lots of false alarms can cause an overlook of real problems or bugs as in Helios case. The system cannot be designed by suppressing some of the negative results, since it would be too risky. Therefore, the only way to minimize the number of residual bugs is to reduce the number of false alarms.

The effect of misleading test results is clear. More than a hundred of root causes for these problems, namely test smells, are defined [11]. In this study, the most common smells in the automation framework are detected. For this purpose, interviews were conducted with the test automation engineers in the organization and maintenance tickets on test management tool were investigated. Most of the assignments were related to the refactoring of a test code which had instable results. Some bugs, which were collected from end users, imply that some scenarios are not covered by test cases. Beyond these examples, prominent cases are summarized in Table II.

TABLE II. Mostly Faced Test Smells In This Study

Test Smells	Description
Duplication	Code Duplication.
Instability & Unreliability	Tests once pass and once fail under same conditions.
Distortive Smells	Tests with Wrong Results.
Complexity	Tests, which are not easy to understand or maintain.
Limited Scope	Tests with insufficient scope.

A. *Duplication*

Code duplication increases maintenance effort and time.

B. *Instable and Unreliable Tests*

1) Flaky Test [11]: Flaky tests sometimes pass and sometimes fail without any change in the system or circumstances [11]. Google statistics [12] provide a clue to guess how much trouble flaky tests introduce to projects:

- 1.5% of all test runs report a "flaky" result.
- Almost 16% of tests have some level of flakiness.
- 84% of the transitions observed from pass to fail involve a flaky test.

2) Suite Dependency: Suite dependency arises when a group of tests pass when they are run independently but fail when more testers run them simultaneously or in a wrong order.

3) Fragile Test: Failure of a test depending on a change of a parameter addresses a fragile test. For instance, test crash due to a test data change implies a data sensitive test.

C. *Distortive Smells*

Distortive smells hide the real results and lead to false alarms or silent horrors. For example, an assertion error can create a pass result even if the expected outcome is not obtained.

D. *Complexity*

1) Eager Test [10] is mainly described in literature as a test which tries to verify lots of features of the same object in a single run. In this case, granularity and traceability are lost, and understandability of tests reduces.

2) Slow tests: The architecture may result in slow or long run time of tests if it is not well-organized.

3) Anti-patterns are the code blocks for which the best practices and standarts are not applied. They may stem from dead fields, bad naming or external resources.

E. Limited Scope

Testing the functionality in a limited scope, e.g., testing only the positive paths, hides the bugs lying under other patterns. Users are warned by messages when there is a misuse. Therefore, testing the functionality for the negative paths are as important as the testing of positive paths.

Another risky situation is related to security. For authentication and authorization functionalities, the positive scenarios test whether the defined users can login to system. However, in this case, the test of the negative scenarios is more important for the prevention of malicious attacks.

Finally, in terms of scope, test data holds a great importance for the coverage. Testers are suggested to use smartly chosen numbers instead of magic numbers.

IV. SOLUTIONS AND RESULTS

With the recognition of the most challenging problems, the strategy to overcome these problems is to determine root causes and to develop solutions against them. This is summarized in Table III.

TABLE III. COUNTER-ACTIONS AGAINST TEST SMELLS

Smell	Root Cause	Solution
Duplication	Same code in lots of classes	Helper Classes
Flaky Results	Async waits	Polling Mechanisms
	They are overlooked and not cured.	Test History
Suite Dependency	Tests are not grouped smartly.	Suites & Annotations
	Executions are dependent.	Clean Up
Fragile Tests	Poor code/architecture	Manual Static Code Analysis
Distorted Results		
Complexity		Static Code Analysis Tools
Limited Scope	Limited Execution Environment	Additional Executions
	Limited Test Data	Test Data Improvement

The solutions proposed in Table III are developed to get rid of test smells and hence to reduce maintenance effort.

Improving test designs and solutions to test smell is as important as determining test smells. In this section, solutions used in our study are presented in detail.

A. Helper Classes

The majority of the test steps are reused in several test scenarios. This introduces the obligation to apply the same fix on at several different points. This is one of the reasons why variations between test classes exist. As test automation framework evolves and number of tests increases, it becomes harder to update the existing code.

Regarding the size of the project, it becomes inevitable to implement and use helper classes after a certain point. Instead of using duplicated code, several test classes call helper methods. Figure 2 shows only a part of the list of tests which use a method from a helper class. For illustration, when a transaction time is updated to 10 seconds, tests as per with 5 seconds will fail. With the use of a helper method, it is sufficient to make this update at a single point only. Otherwise, all classes, which include the wait time, should have been scanned to be updated.

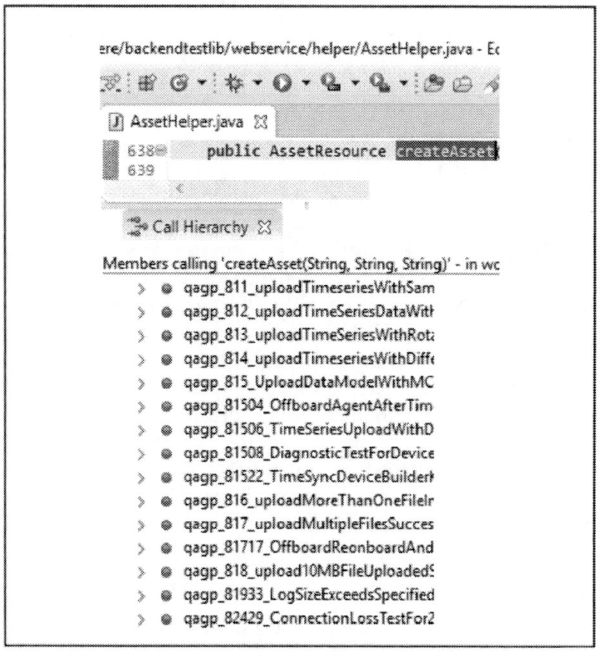

Figure 2. Lots of tests doing the same operation over helper classes.

Additionally, helpers improve the understandability of the code as well, as shown in Figure 3.

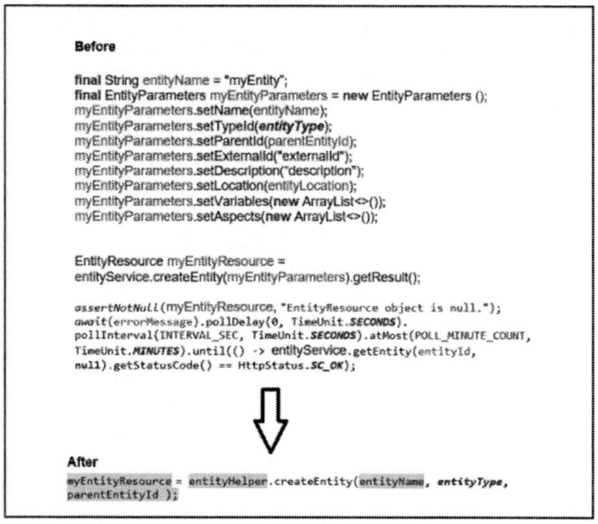

Figure 3. Change in understandability of the code with Helper Classes.

B. Polling Mechanisms

Flaky results are often produced by the methods which do not wait for the result of a call properly. According to a research [12], possible causes of flaky results are collected in Table IV with their frequency.

TABLE IV. POSSIBLE REASONS FOR FLAKY RESULTS

Async Wait	27,08%
IO	22,45%
Concurrency	16,97%
Test Order Dependency	12,42%
Network	9,59%
Time	3,14%
Randomness	2,93%
Resource Leak	2,50%
Floating Point Operation	1,73%
Unordered Collections	1,18%

As suggested in [13], instead of reporting a failure after a single execution, at least the results from three executions are compared to decide whether it is a failure or success. Toward this aim, adaptive retry algorithms are integrated into code.

Test executions are observed before and after applying retry mechanisms to understand their effect. Figure 4 shows the results of 23 consecutive executions. The code without retry failed 6 times, and the code with retry failed only once.

Figure 4. Test results before and after applying retry mechanisms [3].

Figure 5 shows a scenario to illustrate retry mechanisms.

```
00:30:48 request uri =
    "DELETE https://myservice/objects/myobject"
00:30:48 response result =
    Response status of 503 Service Unavailable"
00:30:48 response message =
    "{"errors":"message: Object could not be read."}"
00:30:48 1. retrying process performed because of this
    --> Response status of 503 Service Unavailable"

00:30:58 request uri =
    "DELETE https://myservice/objects/myobject"
00:30:58 response result =
    Response status of 503 Service Unavailable"
00:30:58 response message =
    "{"errors":"message: Object could not be read."}"
00:30:58 2. retrying process performed because of this
    --> Response status of 503 Service Unavailable"

00:31:08 request uri =
    "DELETE https://myservice/objects/myobject"
00:31:08 response result =
    Response status of 204 No Content"
```

Figure 5. Successful response after 3rd request.

A deletion scenario is studied to figure out the working principle of retry mechanisms. In this scenario, "myservice" responds requests coming from end-user and communicates to entity service to save and delete objects. After the receipt of a creation request, the call is responded and the operation is queued. However, if the object is tried to be deleted before the creation finishes, the request is refused since the object cannot be found. This does not address a bug because deletion works when the object exists. In this case, whenever a negative response is returned from the server, the request is retried after a polling duration until the maximum timeout is reached. If the request was not retried, test would fail.

Additionally, polling mechanisms replace static waits. For instance, when an operation is expected to be fulfilled in 2 minutes, even though waiting up to 2-minute-wait is accepted, polling for the result with a certain frequency prevents longer waits after the process is completed.

C. Test History

Against instabilities, scheduled jobs are created over pipelines. Execution of tests multiple times enables us to observe sporadic issues. After each execution, results are automatically reported and instabilities are filtered out at the end. Hence, the risk of overlooking a failure is minimized. A sample representation is shown in Figure 6 [14].

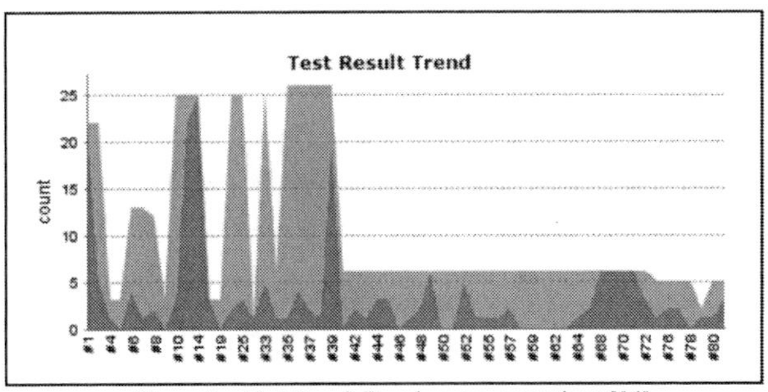

Figure 6. Test Result Trend across executions [14].

D. Test Suites and Annotations

Tests are labeled with annotations to group similar scenarios to execute together. Thus, the whole suite is divided into subsets and by parallel executions durations of the regression testing are decreased. Besides, tests which block each other can be managed in this way to handle suite dependencies. A sample annotation is:

@Test(groups = { TestGroups.***ENTITY***, TestGroups.***DELETE***, TestGroups.***UI*** }, enabled = **true**)

E. Clean Up

Cleaning the created objects after each test execution is of great prominence since otherwise, they result in conflicts in the following executions. Thanks to clean ups integrated in the automation framework, conflicts are not only hindered but also the load on testing environments are also reduced.

F. Reviews

1) Test Definition Review: Test definitions are reviewed by a separate team after their creations. In this way, on one hand, coverage concerns are fulfilled and on the other hand, Eager tests are rearranged.

2) Test Code Review: According to a list of code review standards, test code is reviewed in many aspects by different people, thus the weaknesses in the code are minimized, and quality is enhanced.

a) Cross check: Review of the test design by a second eye reveals smells since a fresh look provides an extra point of view. Fragile codes, false alarm and silent horror cases, scope overlaps, structural smells are treated in this way.

b) Best practices: Removing unnecessary code blocks is observed as one of the most fundamental factors which slow down test executions. A login operation, which is performed over user interface, is a relatively slow operation. Similarly, final modifiers and some other parametric usages affect the memory consumption and execution performance. As a best practice, naming conventions are set to prevent bad naming and obscure tests.

G. Tools Usage

Code quality tools detect smells and advice for the solutions. SonarQube is used in this study to scan test code and to improve quality. Lots of vulnerabilities, such as fragile and long tests, duplicated codes and structural smells, are revealed and fixed by means of these scans. Figure 7 shows that SonarQube warns about magic numbers.

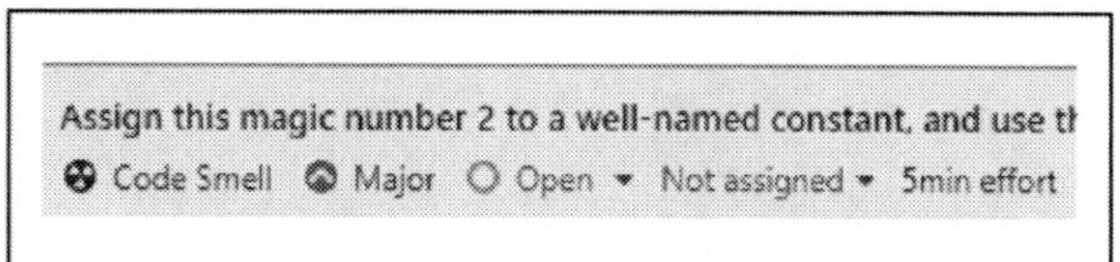

Figure 7. Warnings of SonarQube.

H. Additional Executions

Apart from regression suites and functionality checks, some additional exploratory and compatibility testing are performed to increase test coverage. Some other smells, like Testing Happy Path Only, can be reduced with Exploratory testing. In a sprint, distribution of found bugs over one service is illustrated in Figure 8.

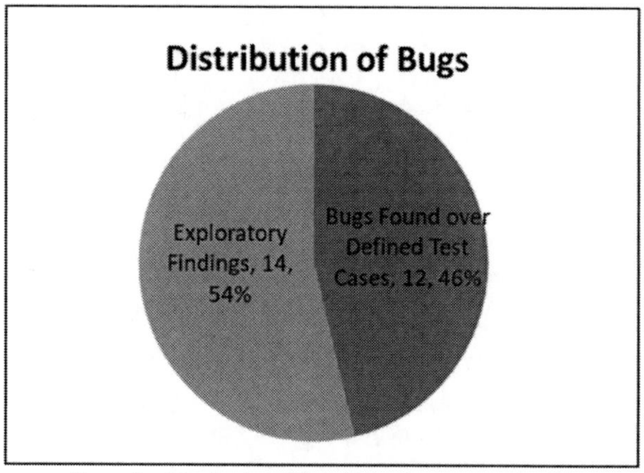

Figure 8. Distribution of found bugs over one service [3].

Therefore, testing different scenarios helps finding hidden bugs. However, there is another limitation beyond scope, which is execution platform. Regardless of the context, running a test only on a single platform limits observation. For instance, verification of user interface functions on a single browser may lead to miss out some bugs appearing on other browsers. To eliminate these risks, cross browser testing is integrated into testing processes with Selenium Grid [15], as shown in Figure 9.

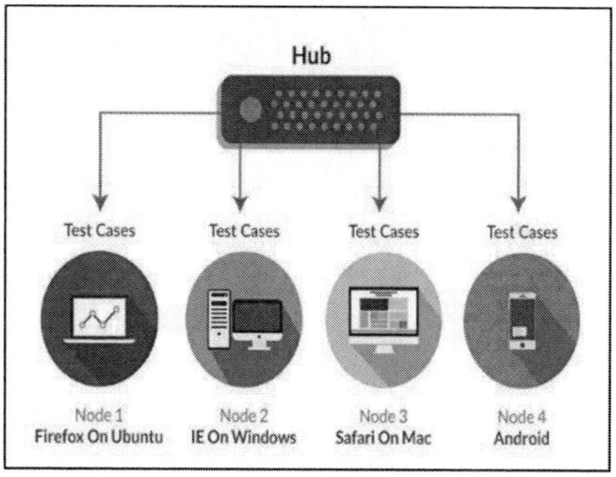

Figure 9. Selenium Grid [15].

In other respects, for hardware tests, a limited number of real devices are available. Thus, a machine manager server is developed in order to increase execution platforms. Upon request, the server prepares a virtual environment for the execution.

I. Test Data Generation

Instead of using static numbers in test data, test data covering different values and corner cases is generated. A piece of code to generate a wide range of data is developed in the framework. Some of the insufficient coverage of scope is resolved with this approach. Figure 10 shows a list of generated test data.

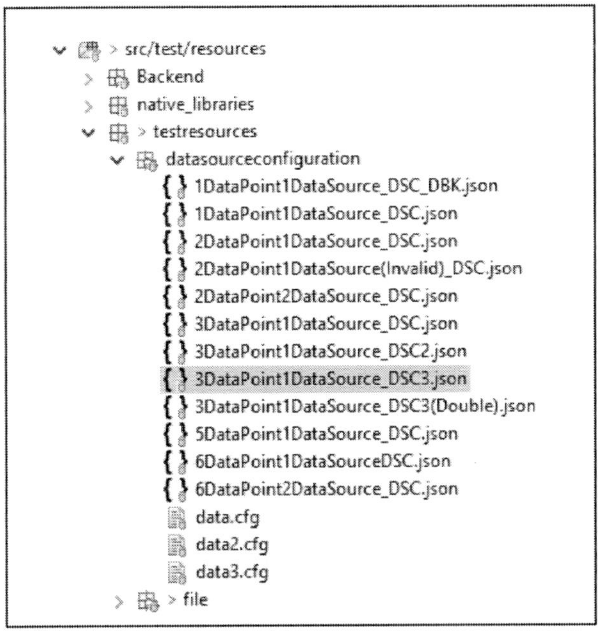

Figure 10. Combinations of test input data.

It should also be noted that spending more effort than needed would be another reason for inefficiency. Several parameters with multiple possible values introduce thousands of test cases. Employing systematic test design methods reduces the number of test cases to a reasonable level. Figure 11 illustrates methods which are used such as Equivalence Class Partitioning [16] and Boundary Value Analysis [16] to determine test input and cover all use cases.

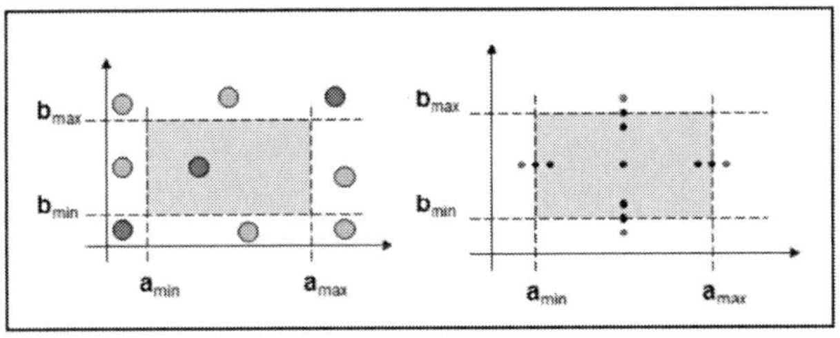

Figure 11. Equivalence Classes and Boundary Conditions.

One of the most stunning examples of test input insufficiency in this study is experienced in the verification of data upload feature. The feature under test works well with integer values whereas the data is lost for whenever double values used. Moreover, user interface crashed when string values were sent. Full functionality is ensured after a careful investigation of test results generated with the use of all possible data types and boundaries.

V. DISCUSSION: CONTRIBUTION AND BENEFITS

In this section, the advantages of explained approaches are presented. However, the risks of implementing counter-actions are also worth being discussed. Implementation of a new mechanism requires some time. Since continuous testing already consumes all resources, reserving extra time for new implementation is not easy. Moreover, regardless of available resources, the effect of the applications is not fully known. For example, refactoring has a risk of code breakage.

Accepting some risks, solutions are implemented to overcome test smells. Several advantages are observed as explained in detailed in Section V. They can be analyzed in the project management triangle of cost, time and scope.

In terms of cost, after the implementation of proposed solutions, effort on maintenance is considerably reduced. Flaky results are reduced and necessity for analysis is decreased. Figure 12 shows how polling mechanisms reduced flaky results.

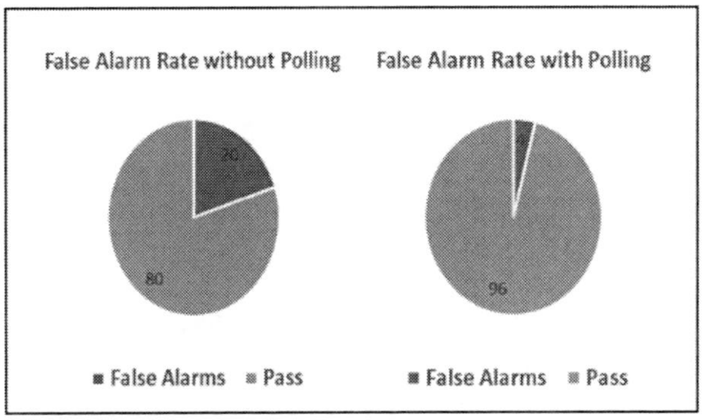

Figure 12. False Alarms Equivalence Classes and Boundary Conditions.

In addition, lines of code are reduced and refactoring effort on those is minimized. Figure 2 gives a snapshot of reuse of simplified and optimized code. One of the most common methods, which is used for an entity creation, is called from various tests 160 times. This means number of lines in code is decreased from 160*N to 160+N.

As far as time is concerned, time is saved in terms of implementation, execution and analysis durations. Improvements lead to rapid automation and adaptation, which in turn is very important since regression testing is needed any time in continuous deployment processes. From the product backlog, it is observed that time spent on implementation of a new test and on analysis to understand the root cause of a failure is reduced thanks to improved debugging and logging structures. In one sprint, 4 out of 16 (25%) tasks were related to refactoring issues such as addition or correction of test steps before application of solutions. Refactoring tasks are not needed any more with the implementation of solutions.

Another advantage of improved scope coverage, bugs are detected in earlier stages of product development and hence the reduced costs.

VI. Conclusion And Future Work

Coping with test smells is a preferential challenge in software lifecycle processes. Minimization of smells has great benefits in terms of cost, time and quality.

In this paper, the necessity for testing and test automation is briefly discussed. The system under test is described. Test smell types are categorized and relative preventive actions are presented. A list of actions taken against test smells is as follows:

- Helper Classes
- Polling Mechanisms
- Test History
- Test Suites & Annotations
- Clean Up
- Static Code Analysis
- Usage of Tools
- Additional Executions
- Test Data Improvement

Eliminating test smells saves a lot in terms of maintenance costs and time pressure. Suggested approaches can be adapted by any organization with a customization according to their work to achieve cost reduction.

As a future work, statistical data will be collected over execution results. Especially, for flaky cases, success/fail ratio and execution duration statistics will be used for further improvements. Moreover, integration of the collected data to artificial intelligence applications on automation framework is on future agenda.

Acknowledgment

I am very grateful to Ms. Berrin Anil Tasdoken who has reviewed the paper and guided me for the improvements.

References

[1] HOW was the Leaning Tower of Pisa stabilized? [Online] Available from: https://leaningtowerpisa.com/facts/how/how-pisa-leaning-tower-was-stabilized/ 2019.11.05

[2] M. Grechanik, Q. Xie, and C. Fu, "Maintaining and evolving GUI-directed test scripts," Proceedings of the 31st International Conference on Software Engineering, 2009, pp. 408-418.

[3] M. Durukal, "How to Ensure Testing Robustness in Microservice Architectures and Cope with Test Smells." International Journal of Scientific Research in Computer Science, Engineering and Information Technology. pp. 167-175, 2019, doi: 10.32628/CSEIT195425.

[4] Microservice Monitoring. [Online] Available from: https://www.appdynamics.com/solutions/microservices/ 2019.11.05

[5] M. Amaral, et al. "Performance Evaluation of Microservices Architectures Using Containers," 2015 IEEE 14th International Symposium on Network Computing and Applications, Cambridge, MA, 2015, pp. 27-34, doi: 10.1109/NCA.2015.49.

[6] G. Bavota, et al. "Are test smells really harmful? An empirical study," Empirical Software Engineering, 2015, 20: pp. 1052-1094, doi: 10.1007/s10664-014-9313-0.

[7] G. Bavota, A. Qusef, R. Oliveto, A. De Lucia, and D. Binkley, "An empirical analysis of the distribution of unit test smells and their impact on software maintenance," 2012 28th IEEE International Conference on Software Maintenance (ICSM), Trento, 2012, pp. 56-65, doi: 10.1109/ICSM.2012.6405253.

[8] A. Vahabzadeh, A. M. Fard, and A. Mesbah, "An empirical study of bugs in test code," 2015 IEEE International Conference on Software Maintenance and Evolution (ICSME), Bremen, 2015, pp. 101-110, doi: 10.1109/ICSM.2015.7332456

[9] What is the cost of a bug? [Online] Available from: https://azevedorafaela.com/2018/04/27/what-is-the-cost-of-a-bug/ 2019.11.05

[10] Analysis shows pilots often ignore Boeing 737 cockpit alarm [Online] Available from: https://www.travelweekly.com/Travel-News/Airline-News/Analysis-shows-pilots-often-ignore-Boeing-737-cockpit-alarm/ 2019.11.05

[11] V. Garousi and B. Küçük, "Smells in software test code: A survey of knowledge in industry and academia." Journal of Systems and Software, 2018, 138, pp. 52-81, doi: 10.1016/j.jss.2017.12.013.

[12] F. Palomba and A. Zaidman, "Does Refactoring of Test Smells Induce Fixing Flaky Tests?," 2017 IEEE International Conference on Software Maintenance and Evolution (ICSME), Shanghai, 2017, pp. 1-12. doi: 10.1109/ICSME.2017.12

[13] Flaky Tests at Google and How We Mitigate Them. [Online] Available from: https://testing.googleblog.com/2016/05/flaky-tests-at-google-and-how-we.html/ 2019.11.05

[14] JUnit Plugin [Online] Available from: https://wiki.jenkins.io/display/JENKINS/JUnit+Plugin/ 2019.11.05

[15] Setting up a Selenium Grid for distributed Selenium testing [Online] Available from: https://www.edureka.co/blog/selenium-grid-tutorial/ 2019.11.05

[16] A. Bhat and S. M. K. Quadri, "Equivalence class partitioning and boundary value analysis-A review." 2015 2nd International Conference on Computing for Sustainable Global Development (INDIACom). IEEE, 2015.

Applying Passive Testing to an Industrial Internet of Things Plant

Marco Grochowski and Stefan Kowalewski
Embedded Software
RWTH Aachen University
Aachen, Germany
Email: {grochowski|kowalewski}@embedded.rwth-aachen.de

Melanie Buchsbaum and Christian Brecher
Laboratory for Machine Tools and Production Engineering
RWTH Aachen University
Aachen, Germany
Email: {m.buchsbaum|c.brecher}@wzl.rwth-aachen.de

***Abstract*—Safety and robustness play a crucial role in the context of the Industrial Internet of Things as autonomous and emergent behavior increase the complexity of Cyber-Physical Production Systems. Given the intractability of exhaustively verifying distributed production systems after modifications, testing and runtime monitoring seem to be two promising methods used to verify correctness in the digitally networked factory. Passive testing and external runtime monitoring are efficient and lightweight techniques that bridge the gap between testing and verification. This paper presents a framework for on-the-fly simulation of a specification relying on the Amazon Web Services Internet of Things architecture and the use of the digital shadow. The feasibility of the proposed architecture is evaluated using an industrial case study.**

Keywords–Passive testing, Industrial Internet of Things, Industrial Cyber-Physical Systems

I. Introduction

The growing demands for individual products and shorter product cycles caused a paradigm shift in manufacturing. The *Industrial Internet of Things* (IIoT) comes with many advancements, but also many challenges. While the technologies in use are well understood, the problem lies in translating applicable science and technology into engineering practice to meet future production needs [1]. The *Internet of Production* (IoP) [2] opens new possibilities for the interaction between different production systems by providing semantically adequate and context-aware data from development, production, and usage in real-time, on an adequate level of granularity. This is a blessing and a curse at the same time as insights gained from the emitted data during production are turned into data that controls the process. Consequently, this yields flexible value chains that are subject to a high degree of reconfigurability and experience an increasing complexity to meet their flexible demands. Beyond that, the data-driven IoP infrastructure, the highly iterative development, and agile manufacturing blur the distinction between design time and runtime, resulting in a lack of formal specifications in functionality, contexts, and constraints as the system is exposed to continuous changes in the environment, which take their tolls on the functional safety and reliability of software. Its validation must go beyond traditional validation using static methods, considering that not all scenarios are predictable during design time, due to the autonomous and emergent behavior.

Testing and runtime monitoring pose two potential approaches to tackle the emerging challenges for verifying the correctness in the digitally networked factory [3]. Based on this premise, this paper combines a specification-based, passive, black-box testing approach paired with runtime monitoring.

A. Approach

The techniques proposed in this paper are applied after the deployment of the system. Figure 1 shows the perception of the IoP and the shift of continuous quality assurance and testing to the operational phase. The systems require either the ability to test themselves while in operation or the existence of a monitoring component that is operated in parallel. Currently, it is not possible to actively test the system during the operational phase as the components are interwoven, and each stimulus may trigger a response which cannot be intercepted. This leads to unwanted side effects and may disturb further process steps of the *System Under Test* (SUT). Furthermore, the system's functionality can not be interrupted arbitrarily during the operational phase (disregarding emergency stop), rendering a reset after each test case execution as infeasible. Because the system is heavily based on the exchange of asynchronous messages, non-deterministic behavior caused by, for instance, latency can complicate active testing and hinder the repeatability. The continuous monitoring and model-based passive testing of safety-critical properties during the operational phase may alleviate the risk of using the system in safety-relevant environments.

Nevertheless, the test cases generated with model-based testing [4] during earlier stages of development can be reused during the operational phase. The formal model from which test cases were derived can be used for passive testing, assuming that the specification used for generation is limited to the input and output behavior of the system.

As passive testing is a black-box testing approach, it relies on meaningful information exchanged between the industrial assets to claim properties about the internal behavior of the black-box. The passive tester runs on an external device, which listens to the communication to extract the relevant messages and therefore does not introduce any disturbances, slowing down the execution speed or interfering with the normal behavior of the system. Its purpose is to passively analyze the input and output behavior of the SUT to detect faults, and it is not intended for intervention.

The runtime monitor acts as a fail-safe, which triggers a safety response upon transitioning into an unsafe region to reduce the impact of the harm. External runtime monitoring is a good fit for closing the gap between testing and verification. It is a lightweight and scalable verification technique that does not necessarily rely on a specification per se but on individual requirements. The requirements and software components can evolve without repercussions on the external runtime monitor, and the physical separation, as with passive testing, guarantees no restrictions in the functionality of the monitored component.

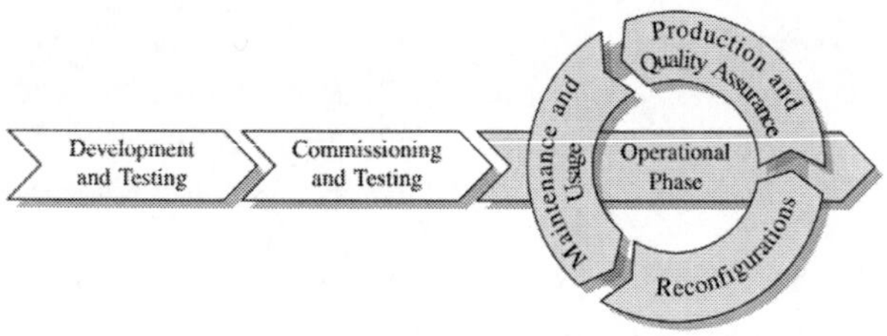

Figure 1. QA and Testing as perceived in the IoP following [3]

B. *Contribution and Outline*

The contribution of this paper is to evaluate the feasibility of a hybrid black-box testing approach for software quality assurance of an industrial case study in which the execution traces are observed, and the specification is assessed on-the-fly.

The remainder of this paper is structured as follows. Section II gives an overview of a related approach and delimits the contributions of this paper. Section III covers the preliminaries and introduces common definitions related to passive testing. Section IV introduces the architecture of the proposed system, shows how the system's behavior is supervised to give insights into the internal states and explains the interplay of the runtime monitor and the passive tester. Section V shows the application of the developed system using an industrial case study. Section VI draws a conclusion and presents future work.

II. Related Work

The contribution is heavily inspired by the work of Salva and Cao [5], yet it differs in many aspects. In their work, a combination of runtime verification and *ioco* passive testing is proposed. Instead of using a classical proxy or middleware to collect traces, they define a non-conformance relation using a formal model based on transition systems for testing a SUT and its specification with a so-called *proxy-monitor*. The proxy-monitor represents an intermediary between the environment and the SUT, which propagates the messages sent between those two entities, whereas the test monitor in this contribution only passively analyzes the traces. Given a specification modeled as an *input-output Symbolic Transition System* (ioSTS), Salva and Cao generate a proxy-monitor to check whether an implementation is ioco-conforming to its specification against a set of safety properties while analyzing the messages using the proxy-tester to detect failures. This contribution, as opposed to the work of Salva and Cao [5], abandons the idea of synthesizing one monitor from the specification and the safety requirement and instead keeps them separate - the focus is put on the specification in this contribution. This allows the specification and safety requirements to evolve and change during the operational phase without requiring a new synthesis of the monitor. For more information regarding the safeguarding of safety requirements during runtime and a brief overview on the related literature, the runtime monitoring algorithm based on requirements written in temporal logic is proposed in [6] by the authors. Further this contribution focuses on the application in an industrial context, whereas Salva and Cao applied their methodologies to the web service compositions deployed in *Platform as a Service* (PaaS) environments. Especially due to the high flexibility in the IIoT and the implications for the *Cyber-Physical Production Systems* (CPPS) this property is desired. Last but not least, the ioSTS model representing the functional behavior of the program is used to generate a monitor to check whether an implementation is ioco-conforming and meets safety properties in the work of Salva and Cao but this contribution directly executes the underlying model with the data from the observations. This leads to the work of Frantzen et al. [7] in which the state space explosion problem is avoided by lifting a test theory for *Labeled Transition Systems* (LTS) to their symbolic counterpart, where the data is treated symbolically. Instead of generating infinitely branching test cases offline as described in [7], the modeled specification in this contribution is unfolded on-the-fly, resulting in an efficient treatment of the possible infinite branching behavior.

Weiglhofer et al. [8] also build upon the *ioco* conformance relation and presented an approach for the selection of test cases using fault-based conformance testing. By mutating the specification syntactically, a fault is modeled at specification level such that the generated test cases fail if an implementation conforms to a faulty specification [8]. In this contribution deviating behavior from the specification is considered as faulty behavior and therefore sink states are introduced explicitly. It has yet to be shown, if the approach by Weiglhofer et al. [8] is a possible alternative to the ideas presented in this contribution regarding the test case selection outlined in the future work. Hierons et al. [9] proposed an algorithm for the construction of a monitor, which is able to handle asynchronous communication between the SUT and the monitor under certain conditions. Instead of operating on the constructed finite automaton the observed trace is used. The asynchronicity is of no concern for the passive testing in this contribution as the data is timestamped and utilized with regards to the event and not the processing time. This allows for more flexibility as delays in the communication are disregarded in the generation of the monitor.

Lima and Faria [10] provide an approach and an architecture that puts the testing of distributed and heterogeneous systems into a larger context. Of particular interest is the hybrid test monitoring approach, which was adopted from Hierons [11]. Hierons showed that multiple independent distributed testers that interact synchronously and a centralized tester that interacts asynchronously with the SUT are incomparable and result in different traces and faults [11]. Currently the techniques in this contribution were applied schematically to one specific processing station. Within this process station the communication was asynchronous and distributed, however the behavior was sequential and hence it was opted for a single tester that interacts synchronously with all the components in the SUT using the event time [11]. When scaling the use case, an approach similar to the one proposed by Lima and Faria [10] shall be considered. Hierons [11] mentions that it is possible to change the hybrid framework by making one of the local testers also act as the centralized tester. Lima and Faria [10] picked up this idea using a set of *Local Test Driving and Monitoring* (LTDM) components and a *Test Communication Manager* (TCM). The evaluation of this architecture is subject to future work of Lima and Faria, however, a similar approach shall be pursued for future work of this contribution.

In the next section, a partial introduction to the theory

behind passive testing is given.

III. Theoretical Background

As transition systems are a well-known formalism to model reactive systems, they are considered as a formal representation for the specification. However, the choice of the semantic model can vary as shown in [12]. A *transition system* TS [13] is a tuple $(S, Act, \rightarrow, I, AP, L)$, where

- S is a set of states,
- Act is a set of actions,
- $\rightarrow \subseteq S \times Act \times S$ is a transition relation,
- $I \subseteq S$ is a set of initial states,
- AP is a set of atomic propositions, and
- $L \colon S \rightarrow 2^{AP}$.

The semantic model as-is currently abstracts from the interactions with the environment. An explicit distinction between actions initiated by the environment and actions initiated by the system is made to account for the asymmetric communication between the system and the environment, following the definition of Tretmans [4]. For modeling the input and output behavior of a transition system, the set of observable actions Act is partitioned into two disjoint sets, an input set Act_I, which denotes the set of actions initiated by the environment, and an output set Act_O, which denotes the set of actions initiated by the system itself, where $Act = Act_I \cup Act_O$ and $Act_I \cap Act_O = \emptyset$. Internal actions, which are unobservable, are all commonly denoted with τ, where $\tau \notin Act$, as fairness is not explicitly considered. Since the components are part of a distributed control system, which uses the network to interact through asymmetric communication, states which have no outgoing output transition are forced to wait for an input from the outside. Therefore it is possible that even though the SUT is composed of determinstic components, the outputs interleave non-determinstically. In addition to the latency of the communication, the aforementioned leads to delays in the occurrence of observations. For formalizing the property of a state in which no output actions are enabled, a special symbol δ, where $\delta \notin Act \cup \{\tau\}$, which is called quiescence is introduced. A state $s \in S$ of a transition system TS is quiescent, if and only if no transition with an output action from s exists, that is, $\forall a \in Act_O \colon \{s' \in S \mid s \xrightarrow{a} s'\} = \emptyset$.

Quiescence is made explicit by introducing self loops with the symbol δ for all states $s \in S$, which do not have an outgoing transition enabled for output actions. It is often useful to consider transition systems where the observable behavior is determinstic. This means that the transition systems have at most one outgoing transition labeled with an action $a \in Act$ per state and hence only one initial state. The determinized transition system, which may serve as a canonical representation, is referred to as the suspension automaton [4].

In order to formally describe the possible behavior of a transition system, the notion of execution fragments is defined. Let $TS = (S, Act, \rightarrow, I, AP, L)$ be a transition system. A *finite execution fragment* ρ of TS is an alternating sequence of states and actions ending with a state $\rho = s_0 a_1 s_1 a_2 \ldots a_n s_n$ such that $s_i \xrightarrow{a_{i+1}} s_{i+1}$ for all $0 \leq i < n$, where $n \geq 0$.

The introduction of the execution fragment gives rise to the formalization of the passive tester. A *passive tester* is modeled as a program graph and is derived from the suspension automaton. In contrast to the proxy-testers from [5], which use symbolic transition systems [14], a slightly deviating definition for modelling the specification is used. A *program graph* PG [13] is a tuple $(Loc, Act, \mathit{Effect}, \rightarrow, Loc_0, g_0)$, where

- Loc is a set of locations and Act is a set of actions,
- $\mathit{Effect} \colon Act \times \mathit{Eval}(Var) \rightarrow \mathit{Eval}(Var)$ is the effect function,
- $\rightarrow \subseteq Loc \times \mathit{Cond}(Var) \times Act \times Loc$ is the conditional transition relation,
- $Loc_0 \subseteq Loc$ is a set of initial locations,
- $g_0 \in \mathit{Cond}(Var)$ is the initial condition.

In order to extract the execution fragments of the program graph, it is assumed to behave like a transition system. Hence, the transition semantics of a program graph $TS(PG)$ over the set Var are given by the tuple $(S, Act, \rightarrow, I, AP, L)$

- $S = Loc \times \mathit{Eval}(Var)$
- $\rightarrow \subseteq S \times Act \times S$

$$\frac{\ell \xrightarrow{g\,:\,a} \ell' \wedge \eta \models g}{\langle \ell, \eta \rangle \xrightarrow{a} \langle \ell', \mathit{Effect}(a, \eta) \rangle} \tag{1}$$

- $I = \{\langle \ell, \eta \rangle \mid \ell \in Loc_0, \eta \models g_0\}$
- $AP = Loc \cup \mathit{Cond}(Var)$
- $L(\langle \ell, \eta \rangle) = \{\ell\} \cup \{g \in \mathit{Cond}(Var) \mid \eta \models g\}$.

To allow the system to make progress autonomously on the actions that it initiates, a formalism is needed in which the environment never refuses the outputs and the system never refuses the inputs by the system's environment. Therefore, the program graph is augmented with a sink state $\bot$, which can be reached from all locations $\ell \in Loc$ by taking a transition with a non-enabled input action

$$\frac{\forall a \in Act_I \colon \ell \xrightarrow{g\,:\,a}\!\!\!\!\!\!/\;\;}{\ell \xrightarrow{g\,:\,a} \bot} \,. \tag{2}$$

Once in the sink state $\bot$, any behavior is possible. This ensures that the program graph is always capable of accepting an action from the environment.

This concludes the introduction of the preliminaries behind passive testing. For details and further information, the reader is referred to the work of Salva and Cao [5] and Frantzen et al. [14].

IV. Adaptation to Industrial Internet of Things

Figure 2 gives a high-level overview of the architecture. The adapter can be seen as a semi-formal interface for transforming the messages passed between the adapter and the SUT into a suitable representation for the test and runtime monitor. In this contribution, the emphasis is put on the test monitor. However, a brief overview of the runtime monitor is given in the following.

The runtime monitor analyzes the execution traces provided via the adapter and concludes a certain property about the SUT. The property of interest is derived from the requirements, which usually originate from the design time and are given in natural language. Requirements describe, for instance, the relationship between two occurring events in which the second event must occur within a given time bound of the occurrence

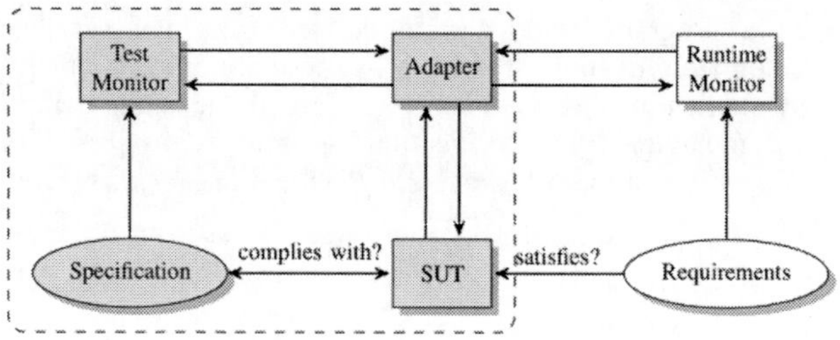

Figure 2. Overview of the architecture.

of the first event. As we only have a black-box view of the system, the possible monitorable requirements are limited to the observable properties. For the use in runtime monitoring, these requirements need to be transformed into formal logic, for instance, using *Metric Temporal Logic* (MTL).

Even though the runtime monitor is able to reason about the future time fragment of MTL, we limit ourselves only to the past fragment, because we can't set any fixed boundaries due to the inaccuracies caused by the asynchronous communication. The runtime monitor currently implements a rudimentary fail-safe, which issues the SUT to halt, neglecting any additional context information, in case of a violation. It was proposed in [6], and the reader is asked to consult the reference for details and further information.

During the execution of the SUT, the test and runtime monitor run in parallel. The runtime monitor is responsible for guaranteeing that the requirements are not violated, whereas the test monitor gives insights into whether the implementation deviates from the specification. The specification describes the behavior of the SUT and is used to derive the program graph for the test monitor, after determinization. The test monitor starts the simulation from the initial state in the transition system described by the program graph of the specification, that is, an initial location $\ell \in Loc_0$ and an initial evaluation η. If a new observation arrives, it is first preprocessed by the corresponding adapter before being passed to the test monitor. The test monitor receives either an input action with its parameters or an output action with the related digital shadow. The test monitor then proceeds with checking whether the program graph is able to make a transition from the current location ℓ_i to the next location ℓ_j with the received action taking the guard and the current evaluation of the variables into consideration. If the transition is possible, the test monitor continues with the simulation. In case ℓ_j is the sink state $\perp$, the test monitor stops the current simulation and saves the execution fragment up to and including ℓ_j for further analysis. It then backtracks to the last location, in which the specification and the SUT were conforming and continues the simulation from there on while logging arbitrary behavior until the initial location is reached again. This is justified by the fact that in case a severe violation occurred, it was hopefully already detected by the accompanying runtime monitor, which put the system into a safe state. Since the execution of a production line usually has a cyclical behavior, the test monitor and the SUT are synchronized in their initial location by (re-)setting the values of the variables. The execution fragment after the backtracking up to the reset is also kept for further analysis. If no observation arrives, the adapter passes a special symbol to the test monitor which is interpreted as quiescence. For practical reasons, a timeout for the observation of quiescence is introduced, such that if in any location a given time bound is exceeded, the program graph is transitioned into the sink state $\perp$. The given time bound may vary from location to location, taking into consideration the specified behavior. Currently, the adapter checks if an observation arrived in the past second, and if this is not the case, the special symbol is issued to the test monitor.

As mentioned earlier, the execution fragments and their simulation results are saved in order to guide the testing process during maintenance or for regression testing. They can be used to prioritize test cases by checking if the execution fragment matches a predefined test case. If that is the case, the test case should receive less importance during the testing process in maintenance as other test cases, which occurred less frequently with the same criticality. Furthermore, using the execution fragments obtained after backtracking, it is possible to investigate whether the test monitor was underspecified for a specific sequence of in- and output observations. The execution fragments that lead to the sink state $\perp$ can be used for debugging and aid the developer to validate the behavior of the SUT after modifying the software by fixing a bug, for instance.

In the next section, first, the case study is introduced. Following that, it is explained how the specifications modeled in a subset of UML and SysML are translated into a program graph used for passive testing, and a brief evaluation of the approach is given.

V. Case Study

The presented approach is validated using an industrial use case, which represents a part of the completion process from a windshield production. It has three processing stations: *Cleaning* (cleaning the windshield), *Priming* (application of a primer), and *Quality Assurance*. The *Cleaning* subprocess was used for evaluation, and it consists of a proximity sensor, a pneumatic suction cup including a valve, a camera, and a robot equipped with a cleaning tool. Each of these components, from now on, referred to as *industrial assets*, has a task-specific *digital shadow*. For further details, the reader is referred to [15].

Figure 3. Overview of the *Cleaning* subprocess.

A. *Digital Shadow*

Even though the term *digital shadow* is ubiquitous, the notion of its concept still differs. The digital shadow comprises task-specific data of the processes, which allows for the reconstruction of the entire life-cycle of an industrial asset [16].

In this case study, Amazon Web Services was used to implement the control of the completion process. The digital shadow serves as a method of data aggregation and refinement for the control of the *Cleaning* subprocess, as shown in Figure 3 by the superordinate shadow service. Each industrial asset uses a digital shadow for its virtual representation and is controlled by an asset driver, which possesses a shadow service that is responsible for the communication with the superordinate shadow service of the entire *Cleaning* subprocess. The industrial assets can communicate locally with each other via the asset drivers using an edge device. All messages are exchanged and transmitted through the use of the *Message Queuing Telemetry Transport* (MQTT) protocol, as shown in Figure 3.

B. *MQTT*

MQTT is a lightweight and asynchronous *machine to machine* (M2M) protocol based on TCP/IP. It offers a 1-to-n connection and three *Quality of Service* (QoS) levels. Unlike request/response protocols such as HTTP, MQTT uses a publish/subscribe pattern of topics via a message broker, which reflect the hierarchical structures of the systems. Each industrial asset was assigned a *shadow/update* topic, to which updates of its digital shadow can be sent. Similarly, other messages with additional information or describing certain actions were defined in [16].

C. *Modeling the Use Case*

The behavior of the SUT is specified using state machines in a subset of UML and SysML as depicted in Figures 4-7. In the following, the workflow of the *Cleaning* subprocess is described. The proximity sensor detects whether a windshield has been inserted into or removed from the workpiece carrier. This information is transferred to the asset driver via I^2C as a 24 V signal if a windshield is in range of the sensor or a 0 V signal if not. The *asset driver* passes this change via MQTT to the superordinate shadow service, as shown in Figure 3. The superordinate shadow service then proceeds with updating the digital shadow and issues a message, if the update was successful, with the corresponding content of the updated digital shadow via the respective *shadow/update/accepted* topic. Figure 4 shows exemplarily the specification of the *Cleaning* subprocess. The focus in the subsequent section is put onto the control process after the proximity sensor has detected a workpiece in the workpiece carrier. All subsequent processes are triggered by the control logic of the *Cleaning* subprocess. As soon as the digital shadow of the proximity sensor indicates that a windshield has been placed in the workpiece carrier, the shadow service of the *Cleaning* subprocess sents a message to open the valve to the pneumatics asset driver using the topic *fpl/cleaner/cleaner_pneumatics*, as illustrated in Figure 5. The asset driver of the pneumatics responds to this message by opening the valve and confirms the change afterward using its shadow service. As soon as the *shadow/update* of the pneumatics is propagated in the shadow service of the superordinated shadow service, the

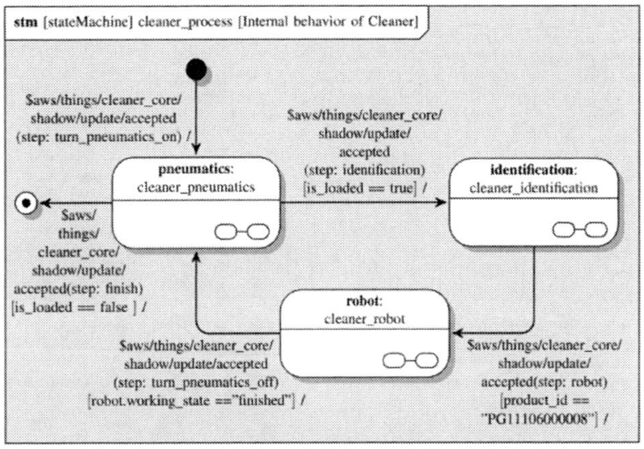

Figure 4. State machine of the *Cleaning* subprocess.

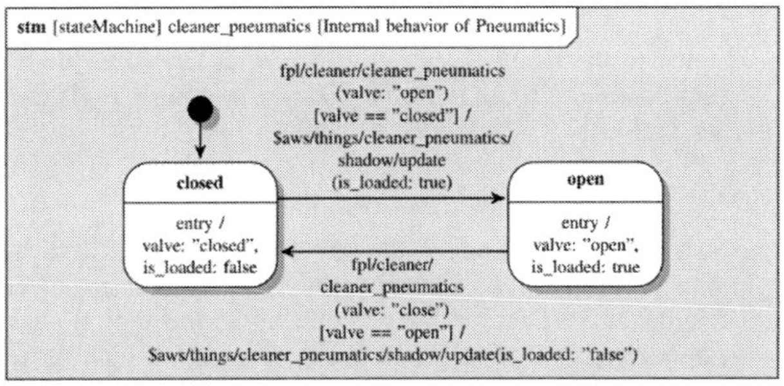

Figure 5. Sub-state machine cleaner_pneumatics of the *Cleaning* subprocess.

control logic triggers the identification step (Figure 6) in which a camera detects the product identifier of the windshield and transfers it back to the control logic. Based on this information, the superordinated shadow service sends a message to the asset driver of the robot to start it (Figure 7). Once the robot has finished and updated its digital shadow, a message is sent to the pneumatic asset driver to close the valve. As soon as the asset driver of the pneumatics received the message and closed the valve, the digital shadow of the *Cleaning* subprocess is

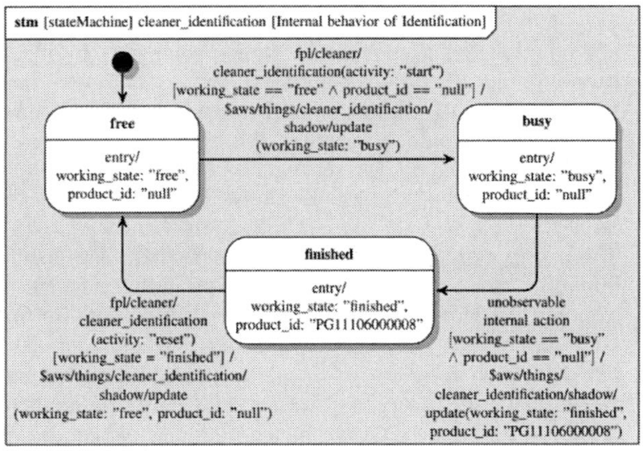

Figure 6. Sub-state machine cleaner_identification of the *Cleaning* subprocess.

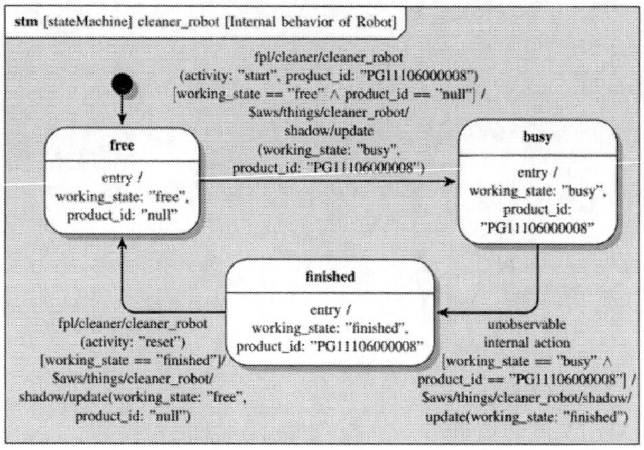

Figure 7. Sub-state machine cleaner_robot of the *Cleaning* subprocess.

updated to the *finished* state. Further, after the windshield has been removed and the proximity sensor no longer registers the windshield, the cell updates its state to *free*.

D. Transformation and Application

The transformation of the specification given in SysML to the program graph used by the test monitor is currently a manual task. The variables occurring in the digital shadow are modeled as atomic propositions $a \in AP$, which serve as invariants in the respective location. The topics of the MQTT messages are mapped to the actions Act of the program graph and are modeled as *signals* with their corresponding properties in SysML. The $shadow/update$ topics are always interpreted as outputs of the SUT, and the $shadow/update/accepted$ messages as input actions. Furthermore, all $fpl/cleaner$ messages are interpreted as input actions. Concretely, the transitions are interpreted as follows: the trigger of a transition is an input action in Act_I, the guard is a guard in $Cond(VAR)$, and the effect is an output action in Act_O. Before a guarded transition is taken, the associated guard is evaluated using the current evaluation of the variables in the source location of the transition.

It is important to note that the signals should not be modeled as in- and outputs at the same time. The message $fpl/cleaner/cleaner\_identification$, for instance, should not be modeled as an output from pneumatics to identification in the *Cleaning* subprocess and as an input in the state machine of cleaner_identification from *free* to *busy*, because that would not reflect the way the messages are passed using AWS. The change of state must take place beforehand, and this can be done, e.g., by the message $\$aws/things/cleaner\_core/shadow/update/accepted$.
The $entry/$ keyword of a state in the SysML state machine implicitly models a $shadow/update/accepted$ message. For example, in Figure 5, the transition from *closed* to *open* with the trigger $fpl/cleaner/cleaner\_pneumatics$ has an output action $shadow/update$ as an effect, which triggers a $shadow/update/accepted$ message in the $entry/$ method of the state *busy* and sets the values of the variables in VAR implicitly on the evaluation derived from the digital shadow.

The experimental evaluation of the hybrid-approach was done on a Raspberry Pi 3 Model B+, which was added as an additional industrial asset beneath the *Cleaning* subprocess. The industrial asset was subscribed to all occurring topics in the specification using the adapter.

E. Results and Insights

The test monitor was able to detect deviations from the specification from the behavior of the SUT at runtime. There were no severe errors, only a few implementation inaccuracies. For instance, cleaner_identification was exposed to a faulty $shadow/update$. The digital shadow was set to *busy* even though cleaner_identification was in the state *finished*, and cleaner_robot was started already. Furthermore, cleaner_robot immediately switches its state from *free* to *finished*. Consequently, the state *busy* was never set in the $shadow/update$. Last but not least, cleaner_pneumatics receives an $activity$: $"start$“ message but isn't implemented with the *free*, *busy* or *finished* concept in mind. The cleaner_process updates its own digital shadow using an internal function of AWS and hence does not send any $shadow/update$ messages. This restricts the set of observable messages to the $shadow/update/accepted$ messages.

VI. Conclusion

It was shown that a specification-based, passive, black-box testing approach paired with runtime monitoring is an appropriate way for improving the quality assurance during operation. While the model-based testing theory describes how to derive test cases, it does not state how to prioritize or select test cases. Therefore, the execution fragments can be used to guide testing during maintenance by prioritizing test cases, which were not observed during runtime or by focusing on the test cases that failed during machine operation. Another benefit of bookkeeping the execution fragments is the possibility to recheck them against a variety of system properties, which have not yet been considered. In the case of machine modification and reconfigurations, the execution fragments can be used in regression testing. Another possibility for the test case selection poses the work of Weiglhofer et al. [8], which uses a fault-based testing technique and can also be applied to the use case from this contribution.

A. Outlook

Currently, the techniques were applied schematically to the *Cleaning* subprocess. Future work shall extend the methodologies to the other subprocesses and also consider their distributed communication. Here, the approaches by Hierons [11] and the concept of Lima and Faria [10] shall be examined.

The runtime monitor currently halts the execution of the system by sending a stop message in case a violation is detected. In some situations, this may lead to damage of the product or the machine. Improved routines could be developed by considering context information such that no harm is caused to the product or machine.
Currently, it is not possible to apply a stimulus to the SUT without affecting other industrial assets. It is expected that testing in idle phases of the process increases reliability. Future work shall enable testing during runtime.

If a deviation from the specified behavior is detected, but the system remains in a state that is not violating, the model of the specification might be underspecified. In this case, appropriate suggestions for updating the model of the specification to improve the quality could be proposed. Furthermore, the derivation of the test monitor from the specification modeled in SysML is currently a manual task, and error-prone, which shall be automated in future work. Last but not least, an evaluation of how well this approach aids in regression testing is pending.

ACKNOWLEDGMENT

The presented research is a work-in-progress in the Cluster of Excellence (CoE) on "Internet of Production" funded by the German Research Foundation DFG. The CoE "Internet of Production" advocates the vision of enabling a new level of cross-domain collaboration between several institutes at the RWTH Aachen University by providing semantically adequate and context-aware data from production, development and usage in real-time, on an adequate level of granularity. The authors would like to thank the German Research Foundation DFG for the kind support within the Cluster of Excellence "Internet of Production" (Project-ID: 390621612).

REFERENCES

[1] S. Jeschke, C. Brecher, H. Song, and D. B. Rawat, Eds., Industrial Internet of Things - Cybermanufacturing Systems, ser. Springer Series in Wireless Technology. Cham: Springer International Publishing, 2017. [Online]. Available: https://doi.org/10.1007/978-3-319-42559-7 [accessed: 2019-10-07]

[2] J. Pennekamp et al., "Towards an Infrastructure Enabling the Internet of Production," in Proceedings of the 2nd IEEE International Conference on Industrial Cyber-Physical Systems (ICPS '19), May 6-9, 2019, Taipei, TW. IEEE, 5 2019, pp. 31–37. [Online]. Available: https://www.comsys.rwth-aachen.de/fileadmin/papers/2019/2019-pennekamp-iop-infrastructure.pdf [accessed: 2019-10-07]

[3] M. Weyrich and A. Zeller, "Testing industry 4.0 systems - how networked systems and industry 4.0 change our understanding of system testing and quality assurance," 4. VDI-Fachtagung mit Fachausstellung, Düsseldorf, Jan. 2016, oral Presentation with Slides. [Online]. Available: https://www.ias.uni-stuttgart.de/en/research/presentations/ [accessed: 2019-10-07]

[4] J. Tretmans, "Model based testing with labelled transition systems," in Formal Methods and Testing, An Outcome of the FORTEST Network, Revised Selected Papers, ser. Lecture Notes in Computer Science, R. M. Hierons, J. P. Bowen, and M. Harman, Eds., vol. 4949. Springer, 2008, pp. 1–38. [Online]. Available: https://doi.org/10.1007/978-3-540-78917-8_1 [accessed: 2019-10-07]

[5] S. Salva and T. Cao, "Proxy-monitor: An integration of runtime verification with passive conformance testing," IJSI, vol. 2, no. 2, 2014, pp. 20–42. [Online]. Available: https://doi.org/10.4018/ijsi.2014040102 [accessed: 2019-10-07]

[6] M. Grochowski, S. Kowalewski, M. Buchsbaum, and C. Brecher, "Applying runtime monitoring to the industrial internet of things," 2019, to appear in IEEE Xplore. [Online]. Available: https://tinyurl.com/etfa2019-preprint [accessed: 2019-10-07]

[7] L. Frantzen, J. Tretmans, and T. A. C. Willemse, "Test generation based on symbolic specifications," in Formal Approaches to Software Testing, 4th International Workshop, FATES 2004, Linz, Austria, September 21, 2004, Revised Selected Papers, ser. Lecture Notes in Computer Science, J. Grabowski and B. Nielsen, Eds., vol. 3395. Springer, 2004, pp. 1–15. [Online]. Available: https://doi.org/10.1007/978-3-540-31848-4_1 [accessed: 2019-10-07]

[8] M. Weiglhofer, B. K. Aichernig, and F. Wotawa, "Fault-based conformance testing in practice," Int. J. Software and Informatics, vol. 3, no. 2-3, 2009, pp. 375–411. [Online]. Available: http://www.ist.tugraz.at/aichernig/publications/papers/ijsi2009.pdf [accessed: 2019-10-07]

[9] R. M. Hierons, M. G. Merayo, and M. Núñez, "An extended framework for passive asynchronous testing," J. Log. Algebr. Meth. Program., vol. 86, no. 1, 2017, pp. 408–424. [Online]. Available: https://doi.org/10.1016/j.jlamp.2016.02.004 [accessed: 2019-10-07]

[10] B. Lima and J. P. Faria, "An approach for automated scenario-based testing of distributed and heterogeneous systems," in ICSOFT-EA 2015 - Proceedings of the 10th International Conference on Software Engineering and Applications, Colmar, Alsace, France, 20-22 July, 2015., P. Lorenz and L. A. Maciaszek, Eds. SciTePress, 2015, pp. 241–250. [Online]. Available: https://doi.org/10.5220/0005558602410250 [accessed: 2019-10-07]

[11] R. M. Hierons, "Combining centralised and distributed testing," ACM Trans. Softw. Eng. Methodol., vol. 24, no. 1, 2014, pp. 5:1–5:29. [Online]. Available: https://doi.org/10.1145/2661296 [accessed: 2019-10-07]

[12] J. Peleska, "Industrial-strength model-based testing - state of the art and current challenges," in Proceedings Eighth Workshop on Model-Based Testing, MBT 2013, Rome, Italy, 17th March 2013., ser. EPTCS, A. K. Petrenko and H. Schlingloff, Eds., vol. 111, 2013, pp. 3–28. [Online]. Available: https://doi.org/10.4204/EPTCS.111.1 [accessed: 2019-10-07]

[13] C. Baier and J. Katoen, Principles of model checking. MIT Press, 2008.

[14] L. Frantzen, J. Tretmans, and T. A. C. Willemse, "A symbolic framework for model-based testing," in Formal Approaches to Software Testing and Runtime Verification, First Combined International Workshops, FATES 2006 and RV 2006, Seattle, WA, USA, August 15-16, 2006, Revised Selected Papers, ser. Lecture Notes in Computer Science, K. Havelund, M. Núñez, G. Rosu, and B. Wolff, Eds., vol. 4262. Springer, 2006, pp. 40–54. [Online]. Available: https://doi.org/10.1007/11940197_3 [accessed: 2019-10-07]

[15] C. Brecher, M. Buchsbaum, and S. Storms, "Control from the cloud: Edge computing, services and digital shadow for automation technologies*," in 2019 International Conference on Robotics and Automation (ICRA), May 2019, pp. 9327–9333. [Online]. Available: https://ieeexplore.ieee.org/abstract/document/8793488 [accessed: 2019-10-07]

[16] C. Brecher, M. Obdenbusch, M. Buchsbaum, T. Buchner, and J. Waltl, "Edge computing and digital shadow: Key technologies for the automation of the future," wt Werkstattstechnik online, vol. 108, no. 5, 2018, pp. 313–318. [Online]. Available: https://publications.rwth-aachen.de/record/726028 [accessed: 2019-10-07]

Low-Code Solution for IoT Testing

Hugo Cunha
Faculty of Engineering,
University of Porto
Porto, Portugal
Email: up201404587@fe.up.pt

João Pascoal Faria
INESC TEC and
Faculty of Engineering,
University of Porto
Porto, Portugal
Email: jpf@fe.up.pt

Bruno Lima
INESC TEC and
Faculty of Engineering,
University of Porto
Porto, Portugal
Email: bruno.lima@fe.up.pt

***Abstract*—In recent years, there has been an increase in the use of Internet of Things (IoT), mostly resulting from the increase in the number of ever-smaller devices being commercialized by different vendors with different purposes. These devices and the ecosystem that they are part of typically are highly complex due to their heterogeneous nature and are typically end-user focused. As a result, testing such systems becomes a challenge, especially when the system logic is configured by end users. To address such challenge, a low-code approach was designed that allows users with no programming, or testing knowledge, to test an IoT scenario with a set of sensors and actuators. This approach has a set of test patterns implemented out-of-the-box so the user simply executes the test suggested by the tool and observes the results. The work was validated in a case study involving a group of users with and without technical knowledge. The results showed that both groups managed to finish the tasks selected with ease. The results obtained during the validation phase with end users affirm that the approach eases the process of testing such systems.**

***Keywords*–Visual Interface; IoT; Integration Testing.**

I. Introduction

Over the last few years, there has been a growth in the usage of Internet of Things (IoT) devices [1]. These small devices have been "turning heads" in terms of robustness, price and general usability [1]. From sensors with the intent of measuring the temperature or humidity of a room to actuators, capable of turning the TV on or adjusting the air conditioning, these devices are taking a leap forward in both technology and also complexity. With the addition of more features and the increasing number of manufacturers providing low-cost solutions which do not provide integration techniques, there is a rising problem - guarantee the correct communication and functioning when grouped together.

One of the areas that is on the rise, regarding IoT, is eHealth, automotive and home automation, or domotics. eHealth is a somewhat recent area that integrates informatics and health in the same domain [2]. In other words, is the possibility of creation of new services in the healthcare domain using the internet. Automotive is also another domain to get certain attention [3]. Lately, a large number of companies are attempting to create autonomous vehicles. These vehicles are expected to not only detect all kinds of road hazards - pedestrians, road signs, traffic lights - but also be able to communicate with the infrastructure. Home automation, or domotics, is an example of an area which is having an increased use in our lives [4] for simple home solutions where, for example, smart sensors, connected to an air conditioning are able to control the temperature of a room.

From the previously observed domains (eHealth and automotive), it is perceptible that errors derived from these activities may cause serious damage to human lives [5]. It is critical that such infrastructures and systems are tested to guarantee its correct functioning. In the case of domotics, it is not such a critical area since it does not deal with human lives directly but, nevertheless if, for example, a door lock is connected to a device that fails to operate it becomes a crucial safety problem.

Another problem that we can point out is the fact that most of the products for such scenarios are developed on different platforms, in different programming languages and manufactured by distinct companies [6]. Communication between such devices may be very hard to establish because of such aspects.

Lastly, the process of testing such complex scenarios is still a difficult task and not everybody can accomplish. In fact, there are already a large number of tools that allow for testing of such devices mentioned, although most of them are proven to be out of the domain we are presenting and are unable to be used by people with low expertise in the area. Most are focused on large-scale systems and require either programming or a high level of technical knowledge to operate.

The rest of the paper is organized as follows: Section II presents the proposed solution; evaluation is described in Section III; related work is presented in Section IV and conclusions and future work are presented in Section V.

II. Proposed Solution

In this section, we present our proposed solution to reduce the expertise needed for a user to test IoT scenarios.

A. Architecture

The developed low-code solution for IoT testing comprises two components: a visual interface (Izinto Frontend in Figure 1) for the configuration of IoT test scenarios, selection of applicable test patterns and visualization of test results; and a second one which is a pattern-based integration testing framework for IoT (Izinto Backend), developed in a previous work [7], responsible for test execution.

The Frontend is a Node.js [8] web application coupled to a diagram design framework, JointJS [9]. The framework allowed for the development of the blocks, links and interaction

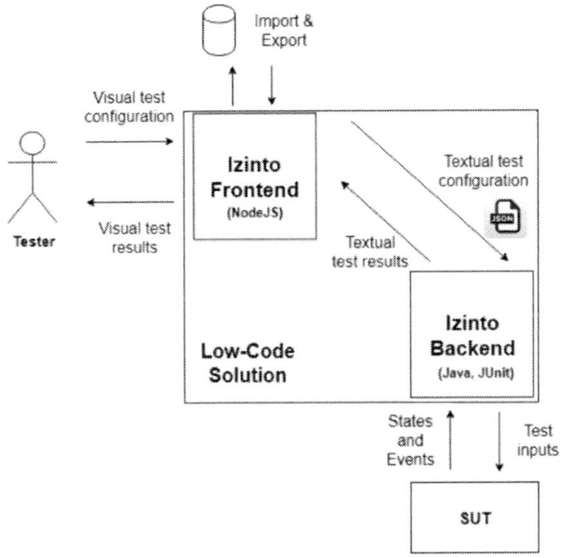

Figure 1. General architecture of the work developed

between them, and the Node.js is responsible to handle server-side events, such as the test execution and test results report.

In the Frontend, the user visually designs the application scenario, its connections and parameters. After that, the tool will suggest test patterns that can be executed and the user chooses the ones desired. Following, the tool will convert the designed scenario into a format the Izinto backend can understand and start its execution. After the tests are executed, the results are reported back on the visual interface so the user can understand what was successful or unsuccessful.

The Izinto backend comprises two main modules: test logic module and IoT components module. The test logic module implements a set of test patterns using JUnit [10]. The IoT module is responsible for the necessary communication with the IoT devices during test execution. As to input data, prior to the starting of the integration test, the Izinto backend interprets a configuration file, in JSON, with the information needed for the application of the test patterns. An excerpt of this file can be observed in Figure 3.

In Figure 1, it is possible to observe the components and flow of our solution.

B. Visual Definition of Test Scenario

In Figure 2 we can observe the user interface of our tool. In this picture, it is possible to distinguish five main parts, or areas, each regarding different functionalities or objectives. In this section, we will focus on the toolbox (1) and workspace (4).

On the left (1), there is the toolbox in which the user can start creating blocks/elements. The blocks are abstractions for physical sensors, actuators, applications and notifications. Each block has a small form for the user to fill in and specify the parameters of the abstraction it represents and also for the test to be executed. In the middle (4), there is the workspace in which the user is able to move, connect and edit the block's properties and test parameters. Figure 2 shows the blocks and links for the running example, as well as a form with the properties of the blocks.

For a better user experience, the tool allows for exporting and importing already designed scenarios as JSON files (5).

C. Test Selection

After describing the application scenario, the user must indicate which tests he/she wishes to execute. In the Test Pattern Arena (2) in Figure 2, there are five test patterns available: action, alert, periodic readings, user triggered readings and actuator.

At this stage, the users select the test patterns to apply. The tool will check which tests the user is able to run, through an algorithm which was developed to suggest test patterns, in regard to the designed scenario. The execution of the algorithm is triggered when there is any change in the workspace and will attempt to find flows that represent one of, or more than one the five available patterns. Once it detects a test pattern able to be executed, it will make it available to run. In the running example, the suggested test pattern is action, since there is a sensor connected to a logic box which is connected to an actuator.

D. Test Execution

When the user presses the test execution button (5), the tool generates a JSON file, similar to the one present in Figure 3. For each test pattern, a different configuration file is generated, although they are all ran at the same time. The Izinto backend will execute the tests by communicating with the devices within the system under testing (sensors, actuators, etc).

E. Visualization of Test Results

Upon test completion, the Izinto backend will return a report in the format of text. Such report will be interpreted by the logic module of the web application and will demonstrate to the user the errors that may have occurred. There are three ways the results are displayed to the user. Firstly, the user will have "drawn" beside each pattern a red cross (in case of failure) or a green checkmark (in case of success), in the Test Pattern Area (2). Secondly, these same figures will be displayed inside each sub-test (each test is divided into smaller and more specific tests). Lastly, the elements of the workspace will be painted green, red or grey in case of success, failure or not tested, accordingly. In Figure 4 we can observe the results of a test which had some failures, but also some successes. In this case, it was executed an action test, which involves a sensor, a logic box and an actuator. As observable, in case of the sensor that performed readings correctly and within delay and deviation set by the user and failures. In case of the actuator, it did not change its internal state upon having received an order to do so by the application, so it is painted as red since it failed.

III. EVALUATION

With the objective of validating the work developed, it was conducted a usability evaluation experiment involving users with the objective of assessing the following research questions:

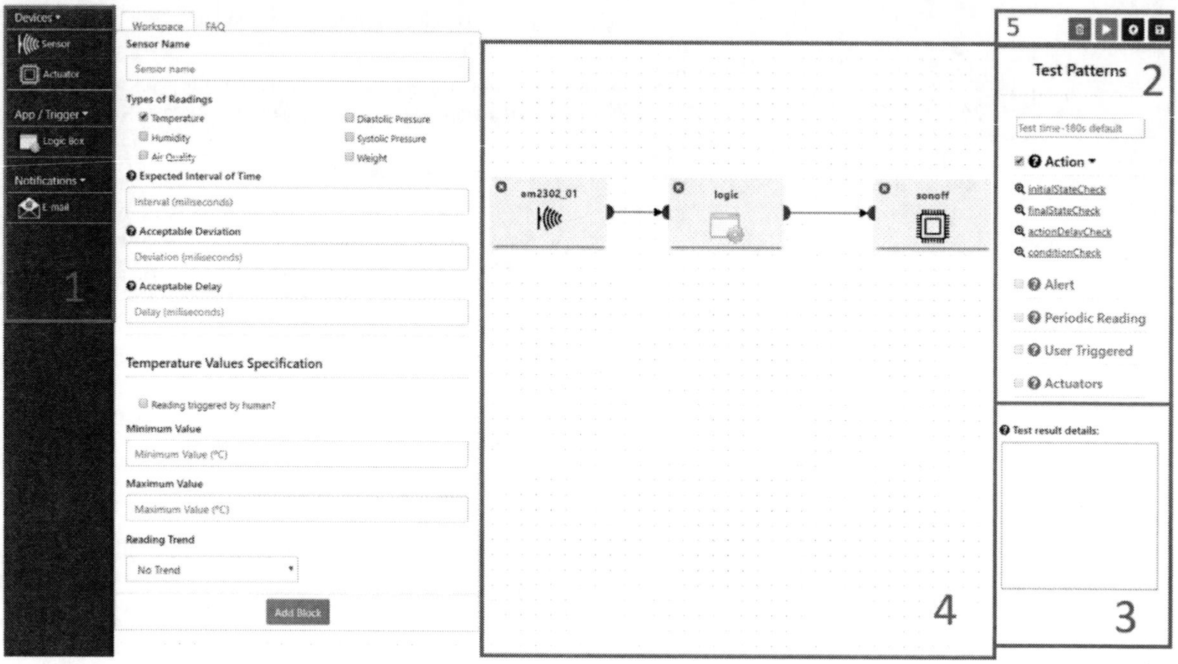

Figure 2. Workspace for scenario definition and pattern test suggestion to be applied to each scenario. The image is already split into the most important parts.


```
{"type": "Sensor",
 "specs": {"id": "AM-2302", "readingSettings":
          [{"type": "Temperature",
            "expectedInterval": 60000,
            "acceptableDeviation": 3000,
            "acceptableDelay": 2000,
            "valueSpecification": {"minimumValue": -40,
                                   "maximumValue": 80}},
           {"type": "Humidity",
            "expectedInterval": 120000,
            "acceptableDeviation": 3000,
            "acceptableDelay": 2000,
            "valueSpecification": {"minimumValue": 0,
                                   "maximumValue": 100}}]
}}
```


Figure 3. Excerpt of a configuration file as input to Izinto Backend.

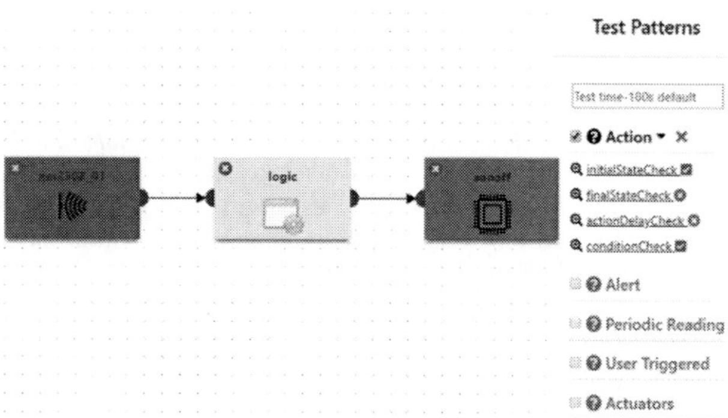

Figure 4. Example of a test result with some successes, but also some failures.

- RQ1: Do users find it easy and pleasant to create and execute automated tests for IoT systems using the developed solution?
- RQ2: Regarding RQ1, are there differences between users with a low and high technical background?
- RQ3: Are users able to quickly create and execute automated tests for IoT systems using the developed solution?
- RQ4: Regarding RQ3, are there differences between users with a low and high technical background?

The metrics used to evaluate were the time per task and the results obtained on a questionnaire made at the end of each task and also at the end of the test. The choosing of participants was split into two parts. In the first, it was selected participants with lower programming and testing knowledge and, secondly, it was gathered users with higher expertise on both areas.

The test was composed of the developed solution and the system under test. The test was executed in a lab which simulates a smart house presented in Figure 5. In this scenario, there is a temperature and humidity sensor, connected to a Raspberry Pi, and a smart socket connected to an air conditioning. Both the socket and the Raspberry Pi are connected to the Wi-Fi of the building. The Raspberry Pi is able to control the temperature of the room and toggle the air conditioning on, or off, as the temperature reaches unwanted values.

The case study involved the execution of five tasks. In the first one, the users only had to import an already set up scenario from the computer and run the available test. Secondly, the user had to test the correct functioning of an actuator. Thirdly, the user would test the correct functioning of the temperature and humidity sensor by running a test of periodic readings. Fourthly, the user would test the triggering of an action when the values read by the sensor would reach certain values, set by

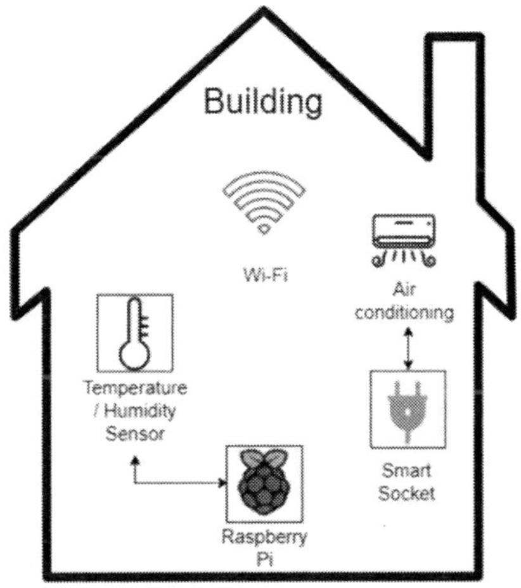

Figure 5. Application example of an IoT system.

the user. The last task had the purpose of testing the triggering of an alert (by sending an e-mail) when the values read by the sensor would reach certain values.

Aggregated in Table I is the data gathered from both the questionnaires at the end of each task and the time per task. The table is split into tasks, one to five, and inside each one, it is possible to observe the scores of both easiness and pleasantness to execute it. Such scores range from one to five, being one very difficult / very unpleasant, and five very easy / very pleasant. On the rightmost column, are present the T-Test values for the difference of the two means [11], regarding each parameter. The differences are not statistically significant (T-Test values greater than 0.05) except one (time to perform the last task).

We can conclude that, based on the results obtained, the visual interface was considered very easy and pleasant to use by both groups of users, allowing to prove RQ1 and RQ2. Also, it is important to point out that, although there is a time difference between the two, that gap is not that big - RQ4. Although, there is a certain time difference between both groups, in general, the times are somewhat small for a task of this nature - RQ3.

The users were also asked to give some feedback regarding the tasks, or the general application. This data was gathered and analysed and most of the suggestions pointed out were implemented. There were also a couple suggestions that were considered as future work.

IV. Related Work

In this section, it will be made reference to existing solutions for IoT regarding both development and testing. It will be made reference to its IoT layer, its test level, test environment, supported platforms, its scope and the presence of a visual interface.

PlatformIO [12]. It is an open-source IDE for IoT development. It supports multiple platforms and a unit testing system. It works on the edge layer and its tests are run within the physical devices. It is a commercial tool and does not possess a visual interface for test configuration. Has support for multiple platforms.

IoTIFY [13]. It is a cloud-based IoT performance testing platform for very large-scale scenarios. IoTIFY works on the Edge, Fog and Cloud layers of IoT and has support for unit, integration and system testing. The test environment in IoTIFY is only for simulated devices. The interface is called "Virtual IoT lab" and enables the user to simulate a virtual hardware lab.

FIT IoT-LAB [14]. It is a very large-scale infrastructure with the purpose of testing a large number of small wireless sensors and other heterogeneous communication devices. It supports layers of IoT Edge, Fog and Cloud and its main purpose is the testing of scenarios and not for the development of IoT solutions. It is both for academic and commercial use and allows unit, integration and system testing. It does feature a visual interface.

MAMMotH [15]. It is a large-scale IoT emulator for mobile connected devices through GPRS. MAMMotH works on all IoT layers and allows for integration and system testing. The connection to the devices is emulated and both the platforms supported and its license are two aspects that remain unknown, although MAMMotH was developed in an academic environment. There is no information regarding the existence of a visual interface.

TOSSIM [16]. It is a wireless sensor network simulator. It was built with the specific goal to simulate TinyOS devices. It is a tool focused on testing, supporting integration one and only support the Edge IoT layer. It was developed in an academic environment and its license is open to be reused. It uses simulated radio connected devices and its graphical user interface (GUI) is optimized for such goal.

SimpleIoTSimulator [17]. It is an IoT Sensor/device simulator that creates test environments with a large number of sensors and gateways. It is a framework with a focus on the integration testing of devices. It is limited to the Edge and Fog IoT layers and there is no information regarding the existence of a visual interface or its domain. It does not use physical devices and there is no information regarding the supported platforms. It is a commercial tool and its license is closed.

MBTAAS [18]. It is an approach that combines Model-Based Testing techniques and service-oriented solutions in a platform that allows IoT testing. Allows for testing across the four levels - Unit, Integration, System and Acceptance and it also features support for all IoT Layers. There is no information regarding the number of supported platforms and it is considered an academic tool. Unfortunately, there is no information regarding its license. It features a visual interface for the selection of tests and results visualization, unfortunately, there is still some expertise required to operate it.

SWE Simulator [19]. It is a tool developed with the intent of representing multiple types and different number of sensors and integrate it with a standard sensor database. It is very much focused on testing of wireless sensor networks and only supports Edge IoT layer. In terms of testing, it only supports system testing and does not use physical devices but simulated ones. It features a GUI but with the objective of monitoring the small wireless sensors' activity. SWE Simulator is a tool developed in an academic environment.

MobIoTSim [20]. It is a mobile IoT simulator to help investigators handle multiple devices and demonstrate IoT

TABLE I. GROUPED TASKS' QUESTIONNAIRES DATA

Tasks	Question	Global Average	Higher Skill AVG	Lower Skill AVG	T-Test
#1	Easiness	4,91	4,88	5,00	**0,351**
	Pleasantness	4,73	4,63	5,00	**0,197**
	Time	0:33	0:29	0:46	**0,063**
#2	Easiness	5,00	5,00	5,00	-
	Pleasantness	4,82	4,75	5,00	**0,17**
	Time	1:46	1:43	1:53	**0,587**
#3	Easiness	5,00	5,00	5,00	-
	Pleasantness	4,82	4,88	4,67	**0,605**
	Time	1:43	1:38	1:55	**0,091**
#4	Easiness	4,91	5,00	4,67	**0,423**
	Pleasantness	4,73	4,75	4,67	**0,837**
	Time	3:58	3:51	4:18	**0,540**
#5	Easiness	5,00	5,00	5,00	-
	Pleasantness	4,91	4,88	5,00	**0,351**
	Time	1:38	1:10	2:52	**0,2e-3**

applications using them. It is a testing framework that focuses on the Fog and Cloud IoT layers and supports integration testing. It was developed in an academic environment and its license is open to reuse. There is no information regarding the number of platforms it supports and the only available visual interface is an Android application so that the tester has access to the values being read by the sensors.

DPWSim [21]. It is a framework that helps developers to implement and test IoT applications by simulating physical devices. Although the team involves one investigator from the commercial scope, it is considered an academic tool. DPWSim works on the Fog and Cloud IoT layers and supports integration testing. It only supports DPWS platforms. Features a visual interface but, unfortunately, only provides managing and simulation support for DPWS devices.

Atomiton IoT Simulator [22]. It is a testing framework that simulates virtual sensors, actuators and devices with unique behaviours, which communicate in unique patterns. It supports all types of test levels and works on every IoT layer. Its license is closed and it features a visual interface but for virtualization of devices. It does not support any forum or community for developers to settle their doubts.

Node-RED [23]. It is a browser-based visual editor that allows a user to connect and wire together online services and API's. It makes use of flow-based editing that makes it visually easy for an average user to create simple, or more advanced, connections between the referred entities. It is not focused on neither testing or developing of IoT solutions but instead a visual interface to connect multiple and diverse services, sensors, actuators, etc.

Easyedge [24]. It is an IoT solution using a low-code approach for the connection of multiple devices without the need for programming. It also possesses a flow-based programming visual interface that enables the user to design their scenario. This platform allows for devices to communicate through the most popular cloud services.

In fact, there are already a large number of tools that provide support for all IoT layers but a few do not allow for integration testing, which is a downside. One of the most important factors we can point out is a large number of closed license tools and the test environment being mostly simulated. Most tools also lack the extensibility needed to work over multiple platforms and most of them are platform-centred. The most crucial point to be evaluated was the existence of a visual interface for easier interaction. We could conclude that most tools did not provide the necessary UI or it was not the most suited for the domain required. Although some are focused on very large-scale systems, there are solutions for smaller and simpler environments. Also, another common issue with such tools is the complexity associated with its use and being mainly focused for experts with very high technical knowledge in the area. There is currently a necessity for tools that allow users from all levels of technical knowledge to test smaller scenarios.

V. Conclusions and Future Work

With the development of this work, it was attempted to reduce the expertise needed for a user to test IoT scenarios. Thereby, a person with no programming, or testing knowledge, can easily test their systems in the most common patterns. Also, we tried to reduce the time a person with higher knowledge would take to test an IoT environment.

In this article, it is made reference to a visual interface with the objective of filling in the existing gap in IoT solutions for people with lower technical skill. Such interface took advantage of an already developed pattern-based testing framework developed on previous work. This interface allows the user to simulate a real scenario, with a set of devices and applications, and perform integration tests with the help of Izinto as an integration testing framework. The visual interface also allows for the visualisation of test results. With such interface, it is aimed to reduce both the time needed for every user to parameterize its test and allow for a larger number of users to test IoT scenarios.

The work was validated with a case study, including users with a distinct level of technical skill. The case study proved that the solution developed was very good. By the data gathered and present in Table I, it is perceptible that even users with no knowledge could complete the tasks. Overall the feedback collected from the users was very good regarding both the easiness of testing an IoT scenario and not needing a high knowledge to use it.

As future work, there are certain factors it is possible to point out, mainly regarding the addition of functionalities to the current work. There are two paths to follow, one with more focus on the addition of functionalities in Izinto and another one by adding more functionalities to the visual interface and better user experience.

In terms of addition of features to Izinto, it is possible to identify a set of new patterns to be added. As of now, Izinto covers the test of features. There are more patterns that can, for example, cover the connectivity, performance, scalability of IoT systems. By covering a greater set of patterns, it is possible to ensure better functioning of such distinct and heterogeneous systems and ensure their integration. There is also the possibility of creating a new set of test patterns for the scope of IoT.

In terms of the visual interface for testing, there is the possibility of creating a module for displaying the sensor readings, or the actuator's state in real time. By doing this, the tester would feel in a more controlled scenario of test and feel in greater contact with the actual values being used for test purpose.

REFERENCES

[1] F. Fernandez and G. C. Pallis, "Opportunities and challenges of the internet of things for healthcare: Systems engineering perspective," in Wireless Mobile Communication and Healthcare (Mobihealth), 2014 EAI 4th International Conference on. IEEE, 2014, pp. 263–266.

[2] B. Farahani, F. Firouzi, V. Chang, M. Badaroglu, N. Constant, and K. Mankodiya, "Towards fog-driven iot ehealth: Promises and challenges of iot in medicine and healthcare," Future Generation Computer Systems, vol. 78, 2018, pp. 659–676.

[3] X. Krasniqi and E. Hajrizi, "Use of iot technology to drive the automotive industry from connected to full autonomous vehicles," IFAC-PapersOnLine, vol. 49, no. 29, 2016, pp. 269–274.

[4] A. Brush, B. Lee, R. Mahajan, S. Agarwal, S. Saroiu, and C. Dixon, "Home automation in the wild: challenges and opportunities," in proceedings of the SIGCHI Conference on Human Factors in Computing Systems. ACM, 2011, pp. 2115–2124.

[5] E. Bringmann and A. Krämer, "Model-based testing of automotive systems," in 2008 1st international conference on software testing, verification, and validation. IEEE, 2008, pp. 485–493.

[6] B. Lima and J. P. Faria, "A survey on testing distributed and heterogeneous systems: The state of the practice," in International Conference on Software Technologies. Springer, 2016, pp. 88–107.

[7] P. M. Pontes, B. Lima, and J. P. Faria, "Izinto: a pattern-based iot testing framework," in Companion Proceedings for the ISSTA/ECOOP 2018 Workshops. ACM, 2018, pp. 125–131.

[8] Node.js, "Node.js," https://nodejs.org/en/, accessed: 2019-05-19.

[9] JointJS, "Jointjs," https://www.jointjs.com/, accessed: 2019-05-19.

[10] T. J. Team, "Junit," https://junit.org/junit5/, accessed: 2019-01-23.

[11] B. L. Welch, "The significance of the difference between two means when the population variances are unequal," Biometrika, vol. 29, no. 3/4, 1938, pp. 350–362.

[12] P. Plus, "Platformio," http://platformio.org/, accessed: 2019-01-20.

[13] T. GmbH, "Iotify," https://iotify.io/, accessed: 2019-01-20.

[14] F. F. I. T. Facility, "Iot-lab," https://www.iot-lab.info/, accessed: 2019-01-21.

[15] V. Looga, Z. Ou, Y. Deng, and A. Yla-Jaaski, "Mammoth: A massive-scale emulation platform for internet of things," in Cloud Computing and Intelligent Systems (CCIS), 2012 IEEE 2nd International Conference on, vol. 3. IEEE, 2012, pp. 1235–1239.

[16] P. Levis, N. Lee, M. Welsh, and D. Culler, "Tossim: Accurate and scalable simulation of entire tinyos applications," in Proceedings of the 1st international conference on Embedded networked sensor systems. ACM, 2003, pp. 126–137.

[17] SimpleSoft, "Simpleiotsimulator," https://www.smplsft.com/, accessed: 2019-01-23.

[18] A. Ahmad, F. Bouquet, E. Fourneret, F. Le Gall, and B. Legeard, "Model-based testing as a service for iot platforms," in International Symposium on Leveraging Applications of Formal Methods. Springer, 2016, pp. 727–742.

[19] P. Giménez, B. Molína, C. E. Palau, and M. Esteve, "Swe simulation and testing for the iot," in Systems, man, and cybernetics (SMC), 2013 IEEE international conference on. IEEE, 2013, pp. 356–361.

[20] T. Pflanzner, A. Kertész, B. Spinnewyn, and S. Latré, "Mobiotsim: towards a mobile iot device simulator," in 2016 IEEE 4th International Conference on Future Internet of Things and Cloud Workshops (FiCloudW). IEEE, 2016, pp. 21–27.

[21] S. N. Han, G. M. Lee, N. Crespi, K. Heo, N. Van Luong, M. Brut, and P. Gatellier, "Dpwsim: A simulation toolkit for iot applications using devices profile for web services," in 2014 IEEE World Forum on Internet of Things (WF-IoT). IEEE, 2014, pp. 544–547.

[22] Atomiton, "Atomiton," http://www.atomiton.com/, accessed: 2019-02-02.

[23] J. Foundation, "Node-red," https://nodered.org/, accessed: 2019-01-23.

[24] Domatica, "easyedge," https://www.easyedge.io/, accessed: 2019-01-20.

How to Adapt Machine Learning into Software Testing

Mesut Durukal
IOT Division
Siemens AS
Istanbul, Turkey
e-mail: mesut.durukal@siemens.com

Abstract—**Software testing cycles have several difficulties, such as coverage of a dense scope in a limited time, due to dynamic product development approaches. Researchers try to use new techniques to overcome these difficulties. This paper presents the utilization of Machine Learning (ML) in software testing stages with its effects and outcomes. Practical applications and advantages are analyzed. The main goal is to make insights about what can be done in different stages of software testing by employing ML and discuss benefits and risks.**

Keywords-artificial intelligence; machine learning; software testing; test automation.

I. Introduction

Nowadays, software applications have very comprehensive features and usages. Most of them interact with other applications and connect to various platforms, which results in a remarkably wide scope and complexity [1].

Comprehensive and competitive features are required for products to survive in the modern world. Products should adapt to new functionalities and be compatible with emerging technologies. On the other hand, they should respond to rapid changes to be one of the firsts in the market and not to be old fashioned.

Figure 1 depicts these challenges by illustrating decreasing delivery time against increasing complexity.

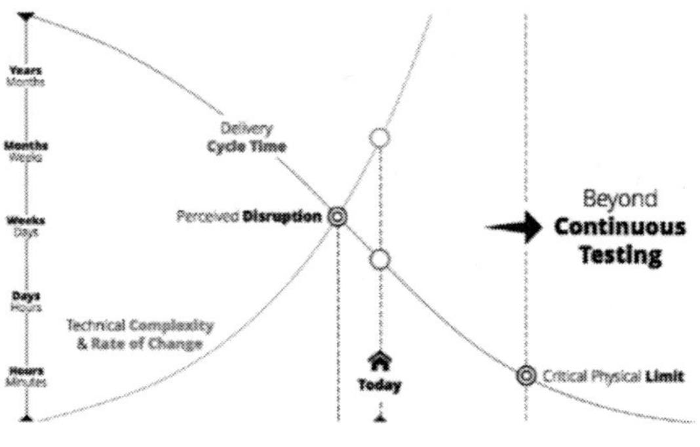

Figure 1. Delivery time versus complexity of products [2].

New challenges in product development have reflections in software testing as well. It is mandatory to take quick actions against gaps introduced by complexity and fast changes in testing cycles. In this manner, new approaches in testing have been applied to overcome these raising challenges. One of the most exciting candidates is the application of machine-based intelligence into testing [3]. ML practices in testing promise for additional coverage and saving on time thanks to their design capable of understanding the system and finding the best patterns. Machines work faster than human beings on analyzing big data and deciding on the most optimum solution. Therefore, faster, better and cheaper processes are expected to be achieved by the usage of ML. Consequently, huge budget will be allocated on adaptation of ML into software lifecycles. Figure 2 exhibits the estimation for ML projects budgets by 2025, which is $90BN.

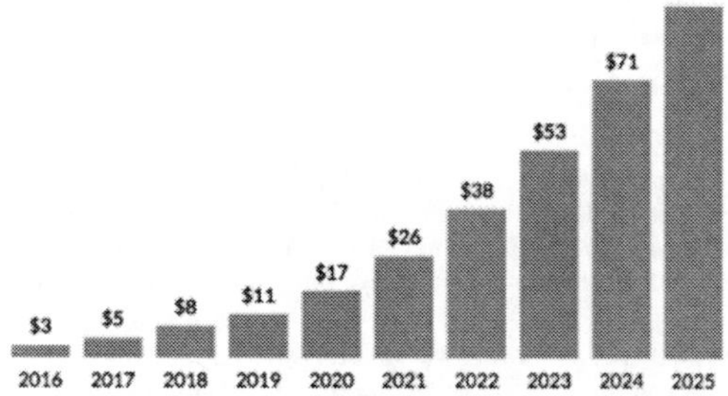

Figure 2. ML Projected Revenue in $ Billion [4].

In this paper, possible ML practices on software testing stages are investigated. Section II describes ML working principles. Section III explains several applications and their outcomes are analyzed in Section IV. Finally, summary of the work is given in Section V.

II. Background

To reduce manual effort, several automation processes are integrated into software development projects. However, human intervention is still needed for the following activities [5]:

- acquiring the knowledge needed to test the system,
- defining testing goals,
- designing and specifying detailed test scenarios,
- writing the test automation scripts,
- executing scenarios that could not be automated,
- analyzing the results to determine threads.

Machines are mainly programmed to follow explicit instructions whereas humans learn a lot through observation and experience. ML is the key factor to fill the gap caused by the difference between the learning processes of machines and humans as much as possible and thereby to reduce human intervention.

ML is defined by Arthur Samuel in 1959 as "the subfield of computer science that gives computers the ability to learn without being explicitly programmed" similar to human beings. If the performance of a machine improves with experiences, it means that it is learning [5].

ML algorithms run in two stages: training and execution. First, machine learns the system, or in other words, it models the system. This stage is called training. Then, the execution is performed by the prediction of next steps according to learnt experiences. In short, what was learned in the past is applied to new data by machines. ML types can be classified as Supervised, Unsupervised, Semi-Supervised and Reinforcement Learning.

A. *Supervised Learning*

Supervised ML algorithms use labeled examples to learn and then to predict future events. Starting from the analysis of a known training dataset, the algorithm builds a model to make predictions about the output values as shown in Figure 3.

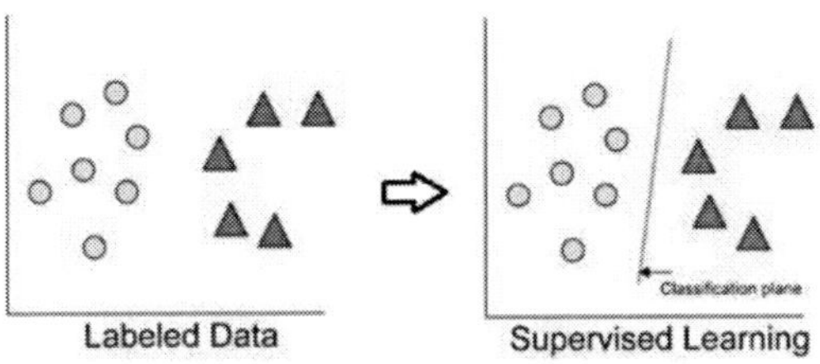

Figure 3. Supervised learning [6].

B. *Unsupervised Learning*

Unsupervised ML algorithms are used when training information is neither classified nor labeled. Under these conditions, system builds a model from unlabeled data to describe a hidden structure. The system is not expected to estimate the right output, but it explores the data, draws outcomes from datasets and finally describes hidden structures from unlabeled data [1].

C. *Semi-supervised Learning*

Semi-supervised ML algorithms fall somewhere in between supervised and unsupervised learning, since they use both labeled and unlabeled data for training. Figure 4 illustrates a sample modeling.

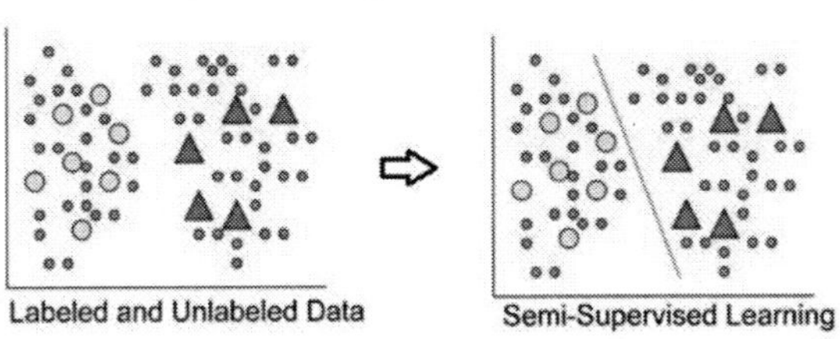

Figure 4. Semi-supervised learning [6].

D. *Reinforcement Learning*

Reinforcement ML algorithm is a learning method that interacts with its environment by producing actions and discovers errors or rewards. Simple reward feedback is required for the machine to learn which action is the best, which is known as the reinforcement signal. Figure 5 exhibits the execution of Reinforcement Learning.

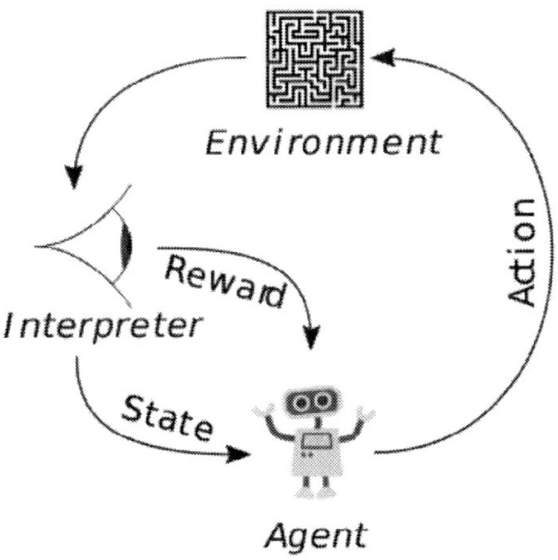

Figure 5. Reinforcement Learning [7].

III. METHODOLOGY

Lots of applications are developed with ML algorithms in various models, such as Artificial Neural Networks (ANN), Support Vector Machines (SVM), k Means Clustering, Random Forest (RF) and k Nearest Neighbors (kNN) as shown in Figure 6.

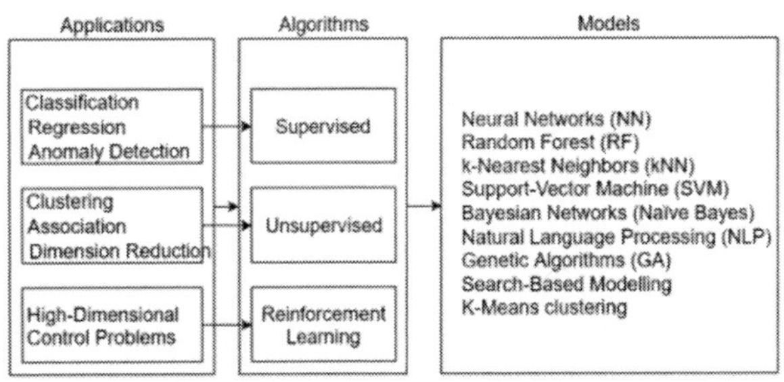

Figure 6. Models to Develop ML algorithms for various applications.

Several applications are developed for software testing purposes as well. As far as the adaptation of ML into Software Testing Life Cycle (STLC) is concerned, the whole process is handled in a structured manner in order to make it easily trackable. STLC is managed in three major stages [8] as shown in Figure 7:

- Definition
- Implementation
- Maintenance

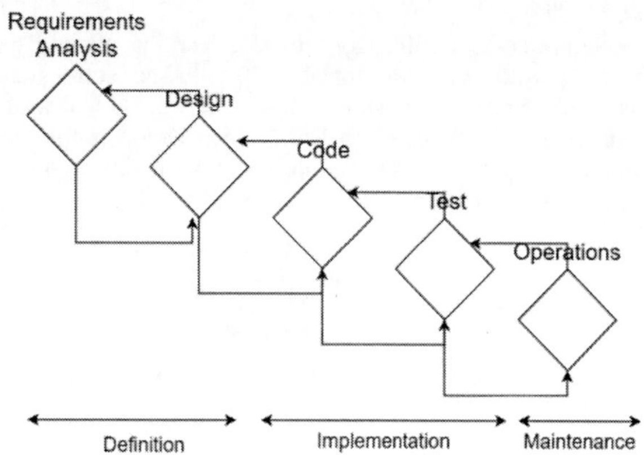

Figure 7. Software Testing Stages [8].

ML is utilized in all of these stages. In Section IV, application methodologies are investigated in detail. Table I summarizes sample tools or models used in the stages.

TABLE I. ML APPLICATIONS IN TESTING

Stage	Application	Tool/Model
Definition	Test Case Generation	AIST [5]
Implementation	Code Generation & Completion	DeepCoder [9]
		TabNine [10]
	Execution	Applitools [11]
Maintenance	Refactoring	DeepCode [12]
	Prioritization	ANN, GA models
	Suite Generation	Search-Based Models
	Bug Handling • Classification • Addressing • Scoring	Naïve Bayes, K-Means clustering models

IV. APPLICATIONS

In this section, ML applications in software testing stages are discussed.

A. *Test Definition*

In this stage, test scenarios are defined to cover all use cases to ensure product quality. ML improves effectiveness and reduces manual effort in the test definition stage in different ways. One of them is letting the machine learn the use cases of the system by observing actions and reactions. In this way, the mandatory parameters and expected inputs are learnt. Similarly, error messages in negative scenarios are also observed. At the end of the learning phase, a model of the system is created. Afterwards, test cases are generated to verify expected results and behaviors according to the model. A commercial example for this approach is Artificial Intelligence (AI) for Software Testing Association (AISTA) [5].

If the working principle is further investigated, it can be understood that the machine observes the responses to requests to model the data structure. Any of the algorithms mentioned in Section III can be applied to generate the model. Then, a set of parameter inference rules are defined to generate the input data required by the test cases [13]. Figure 8 [14] visualizes the model generation.

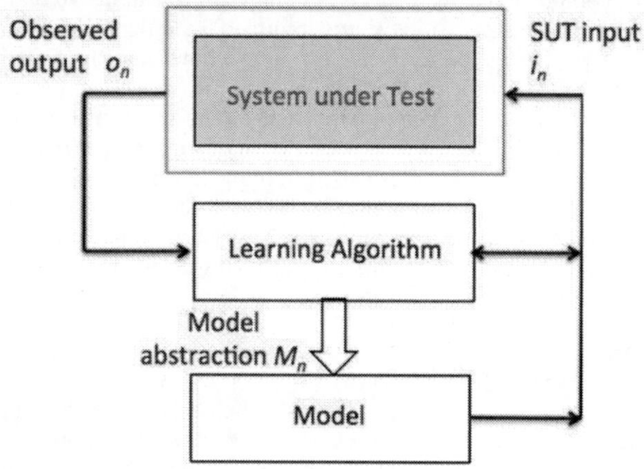

Figure 8. ML based model generation [14].

Offutt et al. [15] followed the same approach to learn the system. They illustrate the algorithm over a sample eXtensible Markup Language (XML) response:

```
<books>
    <book>
            <ISBN>0-672-32374-5</ISBN>
            <price>59.99</price>
            <year>2002</year>
    </book>
    <book>
            <ISBN>0-781-44371-2</ISBN>
            <price>69.99</price>
            <year>2003</year>
    </book>
</books>
```

As the machine trains the behaviors of the system, it learns the fields of entities and supported data types. For instance, after training, the machine knows that a book has properties "ISBN", "price" and "year" in data types "string", "double" and "integer". Finally, test cases are generated by forming request according to this model with perturbated data values. Data values are smartly selected (e.g., boundary values). Table II [15] illustrates a sample set of cases. They constructed 100 test cases, which found 14 faults out of 18, implying that the success rate is 78%.

TABLE II. GENERATED TEST CASES BY MACHINE [15]

Original Value	Perturbated Value	Test Case
<price>59.99</price>	2^{63}-1	Maximum Value
	-2^{63}	Minimum Value
	0	Zero

After the deployments of new features, changes on User Interface (UI) are detected and images removed from the application are noticed. Consequently, the machine starts to learn about the application and relations between the modules. New test cases are generated according to these relations. In summary, whenever there are changes in the system under test, additional test cases are created by means of the approach explained.

It can be concluded that, ML improves the efficiency of testing activities in terms of coverage, time, effort and cost. Instead of analyzing the model and constructing test cases manually, the machine performs these operations. Thus, risks of manual work (e.g., skipping some cases) are minimized.

B. *Implementation*

In continuous testing environments, no one would refuse an increase in test implementation and execution speed. There are many ways to do this.

1) Code Generation & Completion

Coding is one of the biggest tasks in software lifecycles including development and testing activities. Thus, ML is an opportunity to improve or fasten the coding practices.

For robots, a way to write code is, first understanding the problem and then applying the solution. When a problem is defined with inputs and outputs, the needed operations are predicted and the related codes are generated by the machines. DeepCoder [9] follows the same approach. Here is an example of input and output in a scenario, in which negative numbers are filtered and listed in a reserve order after multiplied with 4:

For the input:
[-17, -3, 4, 11, 0, -5, -9, 13, 6, 6, -8, 11]

Expected output is:
[-12, -20, -32, -36, -68]

Figure 9 shows that DeepCoder predicts needed operations after checking inputs and outputs:

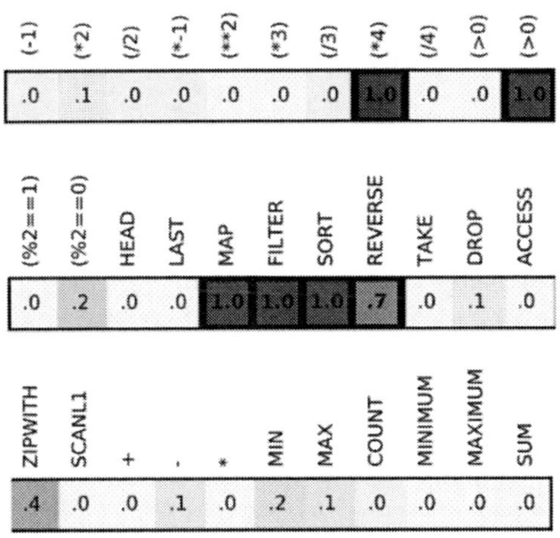

Figure 9. Predicted possibilities of operations [9].

Recognition of patterns between input and output values is achieved by passing them through hidden layers with an ANN model. As a result, they reached a speedup of up to 467 times [9].

Beyond generating a code from scratch, another way to improve the prcess is to automatically complete code. After the patterns the most frequently used are learned, the machines propose the subsequent codes during implementation. As shown in Figure 10, Tabnine [10] is an application, which facilitates test implementation.

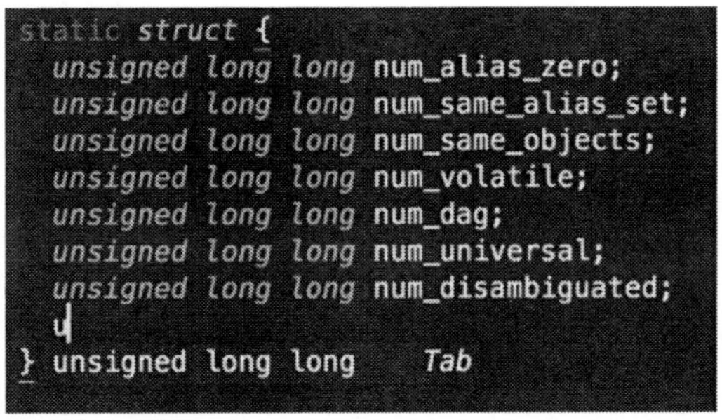

Figure 10. An auto-completion application: Tabnine [10].

In short, ML not only reduces the effort and duration spent on code implementation, but also suggests the most frequently used patterns previously. In this way, standardization is also improved.

2) Execution

In terms of execution, ML helps with:

- Exploratory Testing
- Usability & Efficiency Checks
- Execution Analysis

ML bots perform exploratory testing by clicking every button on the application to test the functionalities. Adam Carmi, co-founder of Applitools [11], states: "We want to make sure that the UI itself looks right to the user and that each UI element appears in the right color, shape, position, and size." ML algorithms are used in their tool Applitools to perform usability and efficiency tests. The system is modeled by the machine according to the defined use cases. Parameters for difficult and easy paths are extracted, and new designs are oriented by these trainings.

Furthermore, execution evaluation is performed by analyzing execution data with ML algorithms. During test executions, ML algorithms learn patterns and user tendencies by collecting data, taking screenshots, downloading the content of web pages and measuring loading times. Then, properties of new features are estimated, and the deviations are detected accordingly. For instance, if loading time of a new page is longer than predicted, a warning is raised. Some outlier detection algorithms are applied with Info Fuzzy Network [16] for ML based test execution purposes.

Results show that algorithms can automatically produce a set of nonredundant test cases covering the most common functional relationships existing in software. A significant saving is achieved from required human effort in this way, which means that benefits of ML are not limited to time only, but also cost and quality.

C. Maintenance

1) Refactoring

According to learnt patterns, some applications like DeepCode [12] propose solutions against code smells. It alerts about critical vulnerabilities needed to be solved in the code. Figure 11 shows how the model of the API is constructed with unsupervised learning algorithms. [17]

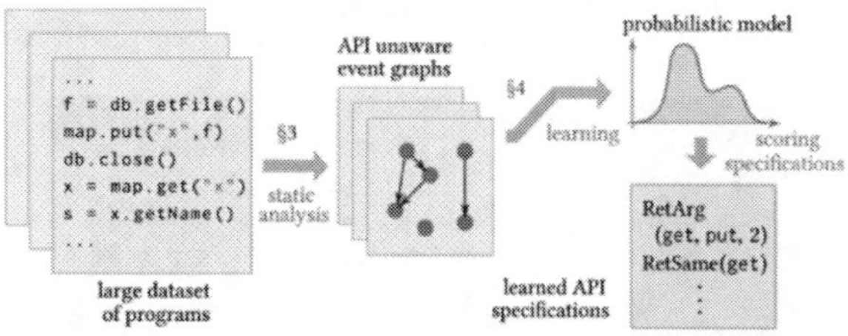

Figure 11. Learning of API Specifications in DeepCode [17].

Bugs are not allowed to go to production thanks to findings. Thus, saving on time is achieved [17].

2) Prioritization

Infinite testing is impossible. With limited resources, prioritization among the test cases has critical importance. Priority is decided according to [18]:

- The probability to find an error,
- Uniqueness in terms of scope,
- Complexity or simplicity,
- Fitness for the regression activity.

For prioritization, test cases are evaluated according to the learnings, which are collected from the labelled training sets. Algorithms are developed with various approaches, such as ANN [19] and Genetic algorithms [GA] [20]. Figure 12 shows how the most significant cases are selected with ANN.

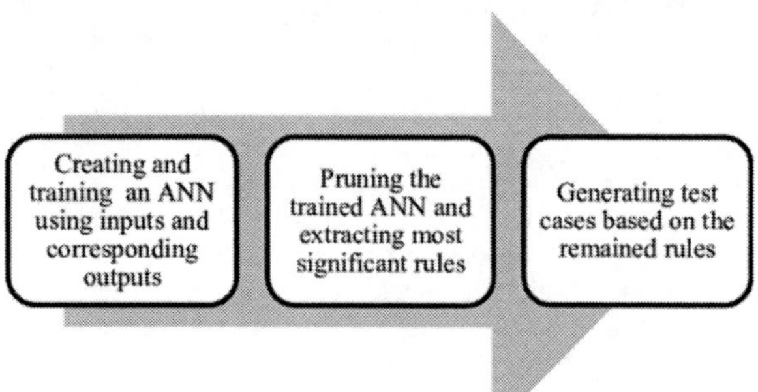

Figure 12. Test prioritization and reduction with ANN [19].

Thanks to prioritization, the number of tests cases to be executed is significantly reduced and less time is consumed on execution. Additionally, adaptation against immediate changes is quickly ensured since regression suite can be generated by ML algorithms.

3) Suite Generation

Whenever there is a change in the software, at least the regression suite is executed. ML algorithms train the relations between the test cases and the features and decide the related test suite for the newly added feature.

It is possible to construct a group of tests, which are similar, by observing the coverages of tests during their executions [21]. The main idea of the analysis performed by the machine is to understand which tests are contextually close enough to each other to construct suites. After the similarities between test case contexts are analyzed, they are grouped by their coverage.

a) Branch Coverage: According to the number of hits to a branch, the algorithm calculates the distances of executions to the target branch and the relation between a test and a branch is estimated.

b) Line Coverage: Distances are calculated with the number of covered lines in the code after the execution of a test.

c) Exception Coverage: Exception coverage is a kind of reinforcement learning and aims to reach as much exceptions as possible. Tests, which throw more exceptions, are rewarded.

d) Method Coverage: Method coverage approach applies the same algorithms over methods. Tests are evaluated according to whether they call methods or not.

4) Bug Handling

Bugs are of great importance since they contain valuable information about the product. According to bugs, useful analysis can be done, such as:

- constructing bug classes in relation with features,
- learning relations between bug contexts and severity,
- learning relations between bug contexts and assignees.

Bug classification provides hints about the weaknesses of the product. For example, if bugs mostly heap together on a feature, some actions can be taken accordingly. In such a case, related tests are prioritized to investigate the feature deeper.

Additionally, scoring of the bugs is very important since they are handled according to their severities. Bugs with the highest severity levels are fixed primarily, then the rest is handled in order. If a critical bug is not scored correctly (e.g., with a low severity), it may be postponed since it is not regarded as a priority. As a result, the regarding fix is not done as soon as the bug identified, which leads to additional costs.

Another point to mention is, for big teams, it is not easy to know each assignee for all features. In such cases, the assignee of a bug can be proposed by the machine according to the previously addressed bugs. Correctly assigned bugs are labeled, and the system is modeled by the machine. Then addresses for next bugs are estimated.

Table III summarizes results from 3 different studies.

TABLE III. ACHIEVEMENTS ON BUG CLASSIFICATION BY ML

Study	Assignment	Scoring
1 [22]	50%	
2 [23]	51.4%	72.5%
3 [24]		72%-98%

To sum up, ML algorithms contribute to bug handling processes, substantially. In terms of quality and scope, coverage is extended by means of the ML observations. If the machines detect any other weakness after bugs' analysis, related test cases are determined and added. Additionally, ML improves the management of bugs, since it helps with correct triage and assignment.

V. RELATED WORK

In this section, an application is discussed on bug severity estimation. For this application, bugs of MindSphere [25] are used. MindSphere is the cloud-based IoT open operating system from Siemens. In the project, bugs are labeled with severity classes:

- Severity 1: Safety
- Severity 2: Critical
- Severity 3: Major
- Severity 4: Minor

Severity 1 is for the cases, which are related to human life and safety issues. Currently, there is not a Severity 1 bug in the project. For the other severity classes, severity assignment to a bug is important in terms of prioritization. Additionally, in the project, Severity 2 bugs are especially tracked, since they are regarded as release blocker issues. Therefore, decision for a bug whether it is Severity 2 or not, affects the progress of the release.

For two different purposes, 889 customer bug entries are collected from Jira. On this data, estimation of a bug severity for 3 classes (Severity: 2,3,4) and decision on a bug whether it is a release blocker or not (Severity 2 or not) are tested. Figure 13 shows the distribution of severity of bugs.

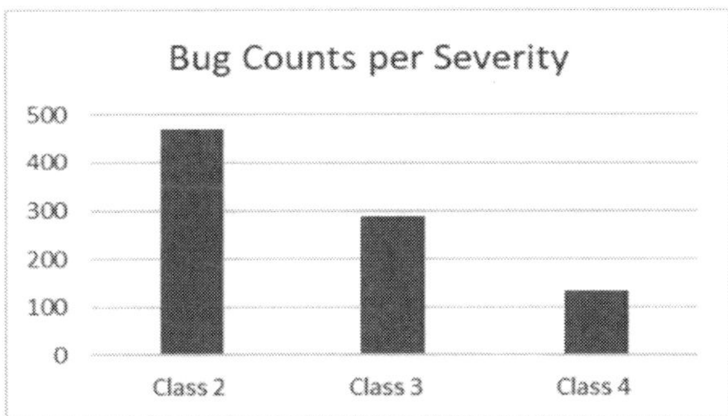

Figure 13. Bug Counts per Severity.

Since the bugs are collected from a real-life project, sample count is not very high. 5% of data is separated for testing and training is performed with SVM on the rest. Figure 14 exhibits the confusion matrix for 3 classes. The accuracy is found to be 64% for this case.

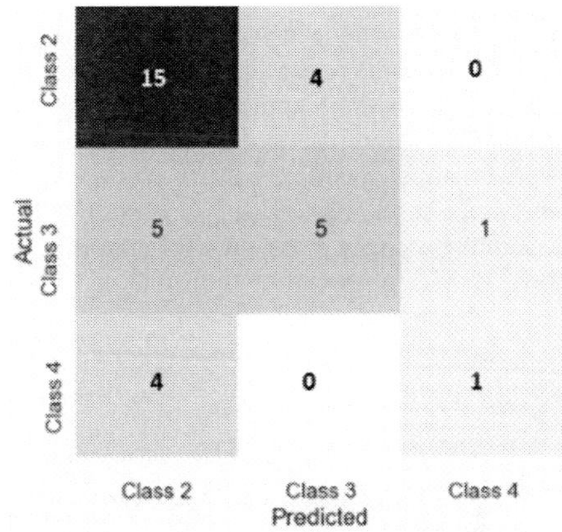

Figure 14. Confusion Matrix for 3 classes.

For two classes (Severity 2 or not), accuracy is 77%. Related confusion matrix can be seen in Figure 15.

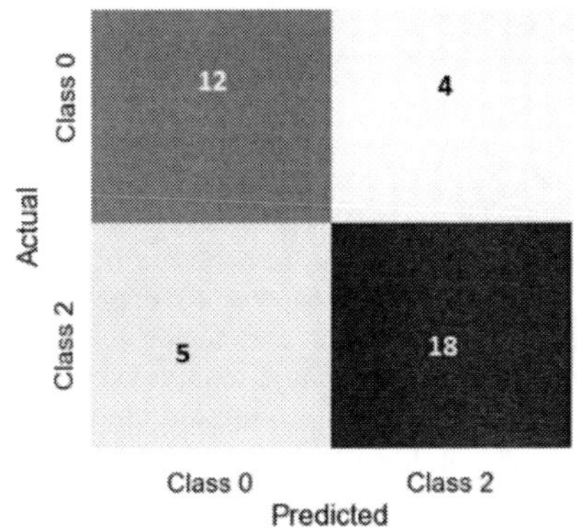

Figure 15. Confusion Matrix for 2 classes.

Severity estimation is not an easy task for bugs. For the same service, a bug can be both Severity 4 and Severity 2. Similarly, the same failure, i.e., data upload failure, can imply different severity levels depending on the conditions or input parameters. Therefore, it is very likely to face difficult decision cases. Considering these challenges, the results can be evaluated as successful.

VI. DISCUSSION

ML is applicable in all stages of software testing cycles. The usage of ML in testing activities has lots of advantages. Test coverage is improved by automatic test generation by machines. For the machine generated test cases, machines' success rate in detecting faults is reported as 78%.

In addition, ML applications provide extra speed in all stages of testing. Compared to humans, machines decide much faster. At least for the rough estimations, AI results can provide a quick feedback. As presented in Section IV, 467 times faster implementation is achieved.

Moreover, manual effort is obviously reduced. Instead of manual tasks, the machines work for defining, executing and maintaining tests. Outliers are detected by algorithms during execution. In this way, the risk off missing bugs is minimized and the cost is reduced with early fixes.

Advantages of ML applications in testing are unneglectable, however, potential risks should not be ignored. Performance, security, control and social risks can be faced in failure cases. Error cases can result in misleading actions, including security risks or fatal consequences [26]. Furthermore, if ML goes out of control, or is abused by people, some ethical and social concerns can arise. In short, it can be concluded that ML is a safe and beneficial tool only when it is under control.

VII. Conclusion And Future Work

Rapidly improving software world grows a great rivalry and creates a pressure on stakeholders in terms of time, cost, scope and quality. Besides development processes, these challenges are faced also during the testing cycles. Thus, any effort that can overcome these challenges is welcomed. In this respect, ML is probably the most promising discipline to improve testing by making better and faster decisions.

Even though it is assumed that ML can never fully replace human beings, it is already surpassing humans in several tasks, such as playing games and providing recommendations. As far as these advances are concerned, the goal is to make use of ML in testing as much as possible.

ML algorithms provide a remarkable benefit on testing activities. It contributes with test coverage improvement, manual effort reduction, better conclusion and addressing.

As a future work, it is aimed to develop an algorithm to support bug assignment. Improving the algorithm for triage is on future agenda and finally, comparison of results with the studies in literature will be performed.

Acknowledgment

I am very grateful to Ms. Berrin Anil Tasdoken who has reviewed the paper and guided me for the improvements.

References

[1] M. Durukal, "Practical Applications of Artificial Intelligence in Software Testing", International Journal of Scientific Research in Computer Science, Engineering and Information Technology (IJSRCSEIT), Volume 5 Issue 4, pp. 198-205, July-August 2019, doi : 10.32628/CSEIT195434.

[2] W. Platz, "What's beyond continuous testing? AI," SD Times, 2017.

[3] W. Murray, P. Karuppiah, and C. Stancombe," On the way to smart, intelligent, and cognitive QA," World Quality Report 2017-18, 9th edition, 2017.

[4] "Which Industries Are Investing in Artificial Intelligence?," Splunk, Priceonomics Data Studio, 2018.

[5] T. King, "AI Driven Testing: A New Era of Test Automation," Japan Symposium on Software Testing JaSST, pp. 1-30, 2019.

[6] A. R. Shah, C. S. Oehmen, and B. Webb-Robertson, "SVM-HUSTLE—an iterative semi-supervised machine learning approach for pairwise protein remote homology detection," Bioinformatics, Volume 24, Issue 6, 15 March 2008, pp. 783–790, doi: 10.1093/bioinformatics/btn028

[7] Reinforcement learning [Online] Available from: https://en.wikipedia.org/wiki/Reinforcement_learning 2019. 11.05

[8] M. M. Lehman, "Programs, life cycles, and laws of software evolution," in Proceedings of the IEEE, vol. 68, no. 9, pp. 1060-1076, Sept. 1980. doi: 10.1109/PROC.1980.11805

[9] M. Balog, A. Gaunt, M. Brockschmidt, S. Nowozin, and D. Tarlow, "DeepCoder: Learning to Write Programs," Proceedings of ICLR'17, March 2017

[10] Tabnine [Online] Available from: https://tabnine.com/ 2019.11.05

[11] Applitools [Online] Available from: https://applitools.com/ 2019. 11.05

[12] DeepCode [Online] Available from: https://www.deepcode.ai/ 2019. 11.05

[13] H. Ed-douibi, J. L. Cánovas Izquierdo and J. Cabot, "Automatic Generation of Test Cases for REST APIs: A Specification-Based Approach," 2018 IEEE 22nd International Enterprise Distributed Object Computing Conference (EDOC), Stockholm, 2018, pp. 181-190. doi: 10.1109/EDOC.2018.00031

[14] K. Meinke and P. Nycander, "Learning-based testing of distributed microservice architectures: Correctness and fault injection," SEFM 2015 Collocated Workshops, pp. 3-10, 2015.

[15] J. Offutt and X. Wuzhi "Generating test cases for web services using data perturbation." ACM SIGSOFT Software Engineering Notes 29.5, pp. 1-10, 2004.

[16] M. Last and M. Freidman, "Black-Box Testing with Info-Fuzzy Networks," World Scientific, City, 2004.

[17] J. Eberhardt, S. Steffen, V. Raychev and M. Vechev, "Unsupervised learning of API aliasing specifications." In Proceedings of the 40th ACM SIGPLAN Conference on Programming Language Design and Implementation, pp. 745-759, 2019.

[18] P. Saraph, M. Last, and A. Kandell, "Test case generation and reduction by automated input-output analysis," Institute of Electrical and Electronics Engineers Inc., City, 2003.

[19] Dr. A. P. Nirmala, Md Shajahan, Somnath K, "Impact of Artificial Intelligence in Software Testing," International Journal of Scientific Research in Computer Science, Engineering and Information Technology (IJSRCSEIT), ISSN : 2456-3307, Volume 3, Issue 3, pp.1519-1526, 2018.

[20] S. Dhawan, K. S. Handa, and R. Kumar, "Optimization of software testing using genetic algorithms," In Proceedings of the 11th WSEAS international conference on Mathematical and computational methods in science and engineering (MACMESE'09), World Scientific and Engineering Academy and Society (WSEAS), pp. 108-112, 2009.

[21] J. M. Rojas, J. Campos, M. Vivanti, G. Fraser, and A. Arcuri, "Combining multiple coverage criteria in search-based unit test generation," Springer International Publishing, Search-Based Software Engineering, volume 9275 of Lecture Notes in Computer Science, pp. 93–108, 2015.

[22] J. Anvik, L. Hiew and G. C. Murphy, "Who should fix this bug?." In Proceedings of the 28th international conference on Software engineering, pp. 361-370, 2006.

[23] V. Stagge, "Categorizing Software Defects using Machine Learning." LU-CS-EX, 2018.

[24] Imran, "Predicting Bug Severity in Open-source Software Systems Using Scalable Machine Learning Techniques." PhD diss., Youngstown State University, 2016.

[25] MindSphere [Online] Available from: https:// https://siemens.mindsphere.io/en/ 2019.11.05

[26] S. Levin and J. C. Wong, "Self-driving Uber kills Arizona woman in first fatal crash involving," The Guardian, March. 19, 2018.

Sandiff: Semantic File Comparator for Continuous Testing of Android Builds

Carlos E. S. Aguiar, Jose B. V. Filho, Agnaldo O. P. Junior,
Rodrigo J. B. Fernandes, Cícero A. L. Pahins
Sidia: Institute of Science and Technology
Manaus, Brazil
Emails: {c.eduardo, jose.vf, agnaldo.j, rodrigo.f, cicero.p}@samsung.com

Abstract—**With ever-larger software development systems consuming more time to perform testing routines, it is necessary to think about approaches that accelerate continuous testing of those systems. This work aims to allow the correlation of semantic modifications with specific *test cases* of complex suites, and based on that correlation, skip time-consuming routines or mount lists of priority routines (*fail-fast*) to improve the productivity of mobile developers and time-sensitive project deliveries and validation. In order to facilitate continuous testing of large projects, we propose Sandiff, a tool that efficiently analyzes semantic modifications of files that impacts domain-specific testing routines of the official Android Test Suite. We validate our approach on a set of real-world and *commercially-available* Android images of a large company that comprises two major versions of the system.**

Keywords–Testing; Validation; Continuous; Tool.

I. Introduction

As software projects get larger, continuous testing becomes critical, but at the same time, difficult and time-consuming. Consider a project with a million files and intermediate artifacts. It is essential that a *test suite* that offers *continuous testing* functionalities performs without creating bottlenecks or impacting project deliveries. However, effectively using continuous integration can be a problem: tests are time-consuming to execute, and by consequence, it is impractical to run complete modules of testing on each build. In these scenarios, it is common that teams lack *time-sensitive* feedback about their code and compromise user experience.

The testing of large software projects is typically bounded to robust test suites. Moreover, the quality of testing and validation of ubiquitous software can directly impact people's life, a company's perceived image, and the relation with its clients. Companies inserted in the Global Software Development (GSD) environment, i.e., with a vast amount of developers cooperating across different regions of the world, tend to design a tedious process of testing and validation that becomes highly time-consuming and impacts the productivity of developers. Moreover, continuous testing is a *de facto* standard in the software industry. During the planning of large projects, it is common to allocate some portion of the development period to design testing routines. Test-Driven Development (TDD) is a well-known process that promotes testing before feature development. Typically, systematic software testing approaches lead to compute and time-intensive tasks.

Sandiff is a tool that helps to reduce the time spent on testing of large Android projects by enabling to skip domain-specific routines based on the comparison of meaningful data without affecting the functionality of the target software. For instance, when comparing two Android Open Source Project (AOSP) builds that were generated in different moments, but with the same source code, build environment and build instructions, the final result is different in byte level (byte-to-byte), but can be semantically equivalent based on its context (meaning). In this case, it is expected that these two builds perform the same. However, the problem is proving it. Our solution relies on how to compare and prove that two AOSP builds are semantically equivalents. Another motivation is the relevance of Sandiff to the continuous testing area, where it can be used to reduce the time to execute the official Android Test Suite (VTS). As our solution provides a list of semantically equivalent files, it is possible to skip tests that validate the behavior provided by these files. Consider the example of Figure 1 in which the official Android Test Suite was executed in a *commercially-available* build based on AOSP. The execution of all modules exceeded 4 hours, compromising developer performance and deliveries.

Suite/Plan	VTS/VTS
Suite/Build	9.0_R9 / 5512091
Host Info	seltest-66 (Linux - 4.15.0-51-generic)
Start Time	Tue Jun 25 16:17:23 AMT 2019
End Time	Tue Jun 25 20:39:46 AMT 2019
Tests Passed	9486
Tests Failed	633
Modules Done	214
Modules Total	214
Security Patch	2019-06-01
Release (SDK)	9 (28)
ABIs	arm64-v8a,armeabi-v7a,armeabi

Figure 1. Summary of the official Android Test Suite – *Vendor Test Suite* (VTS) – of a *commercially-available* AOSP build.

By *comparison of meaningful data*, we mean comparison of sensitive regions of critical files within large software: different from a byte-to-byte comparison, a semantic comparison can identify domain-related changes, i.e., it compares sensitive code paths or *key-value* attributes that can be related to the output of a large software. By *large*, we mean software designed by a vast amount of developers that are inserted in a distributed software development environment whereupon automatic test suits are necessary.

In summary, we present the key research contributions of Sandiff:

- (i) An approach to perform *semantic* comparison and facilitate *continuous testing* of large software projects.
- (ii) An evaluation of the impact of using Sandiff in real-world and *commercially-available* AOSP builds.

Our paper is organized as follows. In Section II, we provide an overview of *binary* comparators and their impact

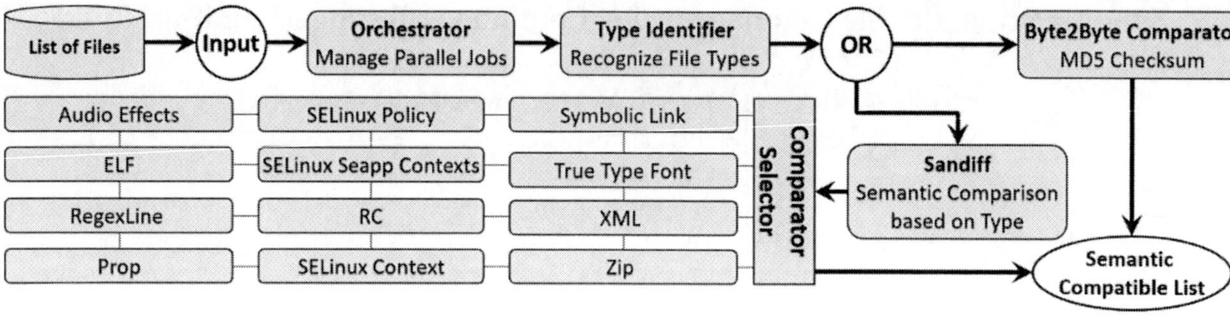

Figure 2. Sandiff verifies the semantic compatibility of two files or directories (list of files) and report their differences.

on continuous testing of large projects. In Section III, we describe Sandiff and its main functionalities: (i) input detection, (ii) content recognition, and (iii) specialized semantic comparison. In Section IV, we present the evaluation of Sandiff in *commercially-available* builds based on AOSP and discuss the impact of continuous testing of those builds. We conclude the paper with avenues for future work in Section V.

II. Related Work

To the best of our knowledge, few approaches in the literature propose *comparison* of files with different formats and types. Most of the comparison tools focus on the comparison based on diff (text or, at most, byte position). Araxis [1] is a well-known commercial tool that performs three types of file comparison: text files, image files, and binary files. For image files, the comparison shows the pixels that have been modified. For binary files, the comparison is performed by identifying the differences in a byte level. Diff-based tools, such as Gnu Diff Tools [2] *diff* and *cmp*, also performs file comparison based on byte-to-byte analysis. The main difference between *diff* and *cmp* is the output: while *diff* reports whether files are different, *cmp* shows the offsets, line numbers and all characters where compared files differs. *VBinDiff* [3] is another diff-inspired tool that displays the files in hexadecimal and ASCII, highlighting the difference between them. Sandiff also supports byte-level comparison, but the semantic comparison is the main focus of the tool in order to facilitate the testing of large software projects since it allows to discard irrelevant differences in the comparison.

Other approaches to the problem of file comparison, in a *semantic* context, typically use the notion of *change or edit distance* [4] [5]. Wang et. al. [4] proposed X-Diff, an algorithm that analyses the structure of a XML file by applying standard *tree-to-tree* correction techniques that focus on performance. Pawlik et. al. [5] also propose a performance-focused algorithm that is based on the edit distance between ordered labelled nodes of a XML tree. Both approaches can be used by Sandiff to improve its XML-based semantic comparator.

III. Sandiff

Sandiff aims to perform comparison of meaningful data of two artifacts (e.g., directories or files) and report a semantic compatible list that indicates modifications that can impact the output of domain-related on continuous testing setups of large projects. In the context of software testing, syntactically different (byte-to-byte) files can be semantically equivalent. Once the characteristics of a context are defined, previously related patterns to this context can define the compatibility

Configuration 1	*Configuration 2*
ro.build.version.preview_sdk=0	ro.build.version.preview_sdk=0
ro.build.version.codename=REL	ro.build.version.codename=REL
ro.build.version.all_codenames=REL	ro.build.version.all_codenames=REL
ro.build.version.release=8.0.0	ro.build.version.security_patch=17-08-05
ro.build.version.security_patch=17-08-05	ro.build.version.release=8.0.0

Figure 3. Example of AOSP configuration files.

between artifacts from different builds. By definition, two artifacts are compatible when the artifact A can be replace the artifact B without losing its functionality or changing its behavior. As each *file type* has its own set of attributes and characteristics, Sandiff employs specialized semantic comparators that are design to support nontrivial circumstances of domain-specific tests. Consider the comparison of AOSP build output directory and its files. Note that the building process of AOSP in different periods of time can generate *similar* outputs (but not byte-to-byte equivalent). Different byte-to-byte artifacts are called syntactically dissimilar and typically require validation and testing routines. However, on the context where these files are used, the position of *key-value* pairs do not impact testing neither software functionality. We define these files as *semantically compatible*, once Sandiff is able to identify them and suggest a list of tests to skip. Take Figure 3 as example. It shows a difference in the position of the last two lines. When comparing them byte-to-byte, this results in syntactically different files. However, on the execution context where these files are used, this is irrelevant, and the alternate position of lines does not change how the functionality works. Thus, the files are semantically compatible.

Sandiff consists of three main functionalities: (i) input detection, (ii) content recognition, and (iii) specialized semantic comparison, as shown in Figure 2. During analysis of directories and files, we can scan *image files* or *archives* that require particular *read* operations. The first step of Sandiff is to identify these files to abstract *file systems* operations used to access the data. This task is performed by the *Input Recognizer*. Then, the *Content Recognizers* and *Comparators* are instantiated. In order to use the correct *Comparator*, Sandiff implements *recognizers* that are responsible to detect supported *file types* and indicate if a file should be ignored or not based on a test context. Once Sandiff detects a valid file, it proceeds to the semantic comparison. The *Comparators* are specialized methods that take into consideration features and characteristics that are able to change the semantic meaning of execution or testing, ignoring irrelevant syntactically differences. Note that the correct analysis of semantic differences is both *file type* and context sensitive. Sandiff implements two operation

TABLE I. SUMMARY OF *CONTENT RECOGNITION* ANALYSIS FOR EACH FILE.

Attribute	Meaning
Tag	Represents a file type
Action	Action to be taken with the file. (COMPARE *or* IGNORE)
Reason	In case of action IGNORE, the reason of ignore
Context	Information about context that is used to define the ACTION

modes: (i) file and (ii) directory-oriented (walkables). In *file-oriented* mode, the input is two valid comparable files, whereas *directory-oriented* is the recursive execution of *file-oriented* mode in parallel, using a mechanism called *Orchestrator*. In the following sections, we describe the functionalities of Sandiff in detail.

A. Content Recognition

To allow the correct selection of *semantic comparators*, Sandiff performs the analysis of file contents by leveraging internal structures and known patterns, i.e., artifact extension, headers, type signatures, and internal rules of AOSP to then summarize the results into (i) tag, (ii) action, (iii) reason, and (iv) context attributes, as shown in Table I. Each attribute helps the *semantic comparators* achieve maximum semantic coverage. To measure the semantic coverage, we gathered the percentage (amount of files) of file types inside vendor.img and created a priority list to develop semantic comparators. For instance, both ELF (32 and 64 bits) files represent about 60% of total files inside .img files, whereas symbolic link files about 14% and XML files about 6%. This process enables us to achieve about 90% of semantic coverage. As the comparison is performed in a semantic mode, it is necessary to know the context in which the artifact was used to enable the correlation between files and test cases. Note that a file can impact one or more tests in a different manner, e.g., *performance*, *security* and *fuzz* tests. The remaining 10% of files are compared using the byte-to-byte comparator.

Each *recognizer* returns a unique tag from a set of known tags, or a tag with no content to indicate that the file could not be recognized. Recognizers can also decide whether a file should be ignored based on context by using the *action attribute* and indicating a justification in the *reason attribute*. Recognizers are evaluated sequentially. The first recognizer runs and tries to tag the file: if the file cannot be tagged, the next recognizer in the list is called, repeating this process until a valid recognizer is found or, in the latter case, the file is tagged to the *default comparator* (byte-to-byte). Table II summarizes the list of AOSP-based recognizers supported by Sandiff.

B. Semantic Comparators

Sandiff was designed to maximize semantic coverage of the AOSP by supporting the most relevant intermediate files used for packing artifacts into `.img` image files, i.e., the bootable binaries used to perform factory reset and restore original operational system of AOSP-based devices. To ensure the approach assertiveness, for each semantic comparator, we performed an exploratory data analysis over each file type and use case to define patterns of the context's characteristics. The exploratory data analysis over each file type relies on

TABLE II. LIST OF AOSP-BASED *RECOGNIZERS* SUPPORTED BY SANDIFF.

Recognizer	Tags	Action
IgnoredByContextRecognizer	ignored_by_context	Ingore
ContextFileRecognizer	zip_manifest	Compare
MagicRecognizer	elf, zip, xml, ttf, sepolicy, empty	Compare
AudioEffectsRecognizer	audio_effects_format	Compare
SeappContextsRecognizerc	seapp_contexts	Compare
PKCS7Recognizer	pkcs7	Compare
PropRecognizer	prop	Compare
RegexLineRecognizer	regex_line	Compare
SEContextRecognizer	secontext	Compare
ExtensionRecognizer	Based on file name. e.g.: file.jpg ? "jpg"	Compare

three steps: (i) file type study, (ii) where these files are used, and (iii) how these files are used (knowledge of its behavior). The result of this analysis was used to implement each semantic comparator. The following subsections describe the main comparators of Sandiff.

1) Checksum: Performs byte-to-byte (checksum) comparison and is the default comparator for binary files (e.g., *bin*, *tlbin*, *dat*) and for cases where file type is not recognized or unsupported. Sandiff employs the industry standard [6] MD5 checksum algorithm, but also offers a set of alternative algorithms that can be set manually by the user: SHA1, SHA224, SHA256, SHA384, SHA512.

2) Audio Effects: AOSP represents audio effects and configurations in `.conf` files that are similar to `.xml`:

(i) `<name>{[sub-elements]}`

(ii) `<name> <value>`

Audio files are analyzed by an ordered model detection algorithm that represents each element (and its sub-elements) as nodes in a tree that is alphabetically sorted.

3) Executable and Linking Format (ELF): ELF files are common containers for binary files in Unix-base systems that packs object code, shared libraries, and core dumps. This comparator uses the definition of the ELF format (`<elf.h>` library) to analyze (i) the files architecture (32 or 64-bit), (ii) the object file type, (iii) the number of section entries in header, (iv) the number of symbols on *.symtab* and *.dynsym* sections, and (v) the mapping of segments to sections by comparing program headers content. To correlate sections to *test cases*, Sandiff detects semantic differences for AOSP *test-sensitive* sections (e.g., *.bss*, *.rodata*, *.symtab*, *.dynsym*, *.text*). When ELF files are Linux loadable kernel modules (.ko extension, kernel object), the comparator checks if the module signature is present to compare its size and values.

4) ListComparator: Compares files structured as list of items, reporting (i) items that exists only in one of the compared files, (ii) line displacements (lines in different positions), and (iv) duplicated lines. To facilitate the correlation between files and *test cases*, Sandiff implements specific semantic comparators for *Prop*, *Regex Line* and *SELinux* files, as they contain properties and settings that are specific to a particular AOSP-based device or vendor.

a) Prop: Supports files with `.prop` extensions and with `<key> = <value>` patterns. Prior to analysis, each line of a *.prop* file is categorized in *import*, *include* or *property*, as defined below:

(i) *import*: lines with format `import <key>`.
(ii) *include*: lines with format `include <key>`.
(iii) *property*: lines with format `<key> = [<value>]`.

After categorization, each line is added to its respective list. The comparator provides a list of properties to be discarded (considered irrelevant) on the semantic comparison. A line can be ignored if is empty or commented.

b) RegexLine: Performs the comparison of files in which all lines match a user-defined regex pattern, e.g., `'/system/.'` or `'.so'`, offering the flexibility to perform semantic comparison of unusual files.

c) SELinux: Security-Enhanced Linux, or SELinux, is a mechanism that implements Mandatory Access Control (MAC) in Linux kernel to control the permissions a subject context has over a target object, representing an important security feature for modern Linux-based systems. Sandiff supports semantic comparison of SELinux specification files that are relevant to *security test cases* of the VTS suite, i.e., *Seapp contexts*, *SELinux context*, and *SELinux Policy*, summarizing (i) components, (ii) type enforcement rules, (iii) RBAC rules, (iv) MLS rules, (v) constraints, and (vi) labeling statements.

5) RC: The Android Init System is responsible for the AOSP bootup sequence and is related to the bootloader, *init* and *init* resources, components that are typically customized for specific AOSP-based devices and vendors. The initialization of modern systems consists of several phases that can impact a myriad number of *test cases* (e.g., *kernel*, *performance*, *fuzz*, *security*). Sandiff supports the semantic comparison of `.rc` files that contain instructions used by the *init* system: *actions*, *commands*, *services*, *options*, and *imports*.

6) Symbolic Link: The semantic comparison of symbolic links is an important feature of Sandiff that allows correlation between *test cases* and absolute or relative paths that can be differently stored across specific AOSP-based devices or vendors, but result in the same output or execution. The algorithm is defined as follows: first it checks if the file status is a symbolic link, and if so, reads where it points to. With this content it verifies if two compared symbolic links points to same path. The library used to check the file status depends on the input type and is abstracted by *Input Recognizers*. Take the following instances as examples:

File System → `<sys/stat.h>`
Image File → `<ext2/ext2fs.h>`
ZIP → `<zip.h>`

7) True Type Font: Sandiff uses the Freetype library [7] to extract data from TrueType fonts, which are modeled in terms of faces and tables properties. For each property field, the comparator tags the *semantically* irrelevant sections to ignore during semantic comparison. This is a crucial feature of Sandiff since is common that vendors design different customizations on top of the default AOSP user interface and experience.

8) XML: XML is the *de facto* standard format for web publishing and data transportation, being used across all modules of AOSP. To support the semantic comparison of XML files, Sandiff uses the well-known *Xerces* library [8] by parsing the Document Object Model (DOM), ensuring robustness to complex hierarchies. The algorithm compares nodes and checks if they have (i) different attributes length, (ii) different values, (iii) attributes are only in one of the inputs, and (iv) different child nodes (added or removed).

9) Zip and Zip Manifest: During the building process of AOSP images, zip-based files may contain Java Archives (.jar), Android Packages (.apk) or ZIP files itself (.zip). As these files follows the ZIP structure, they are analyzed by the same semantic comparator. Note that, due to the *archive* nature of ZIP format, Sandiff covers different cases:

(i) *In-place*: there is no need to extract files.
(ii) *Ignore metadata*: ignore metadata that is related to the ZIP specification, e.g., archive creation time and archive modification time.
(iii) *Recursive*: files inside ZIP are individually processed by Sandiff, so they can be handled by the proper *semantic comparator*. The results are summarized to represent the analysis of the zip archive.

Another important class of files of the AOSP building process are the *ZIP manifests*. Manifest files can contain properties that are time-dependent, impacting *naive* byte-to-byte comparators. Sandiff supports the semantic comparison of *manifests* by ignoring *header* keys entries (e.g., String: "Created-By", Regex: "(.+)-Digest") and *files* keys entries (e.g., SEC-INF/buildinfo.xml).

10) PKCS7: Public Key Cryptography Standards, or PKCS, are a group of public-key cryptography standards that is used by AOSP to sign and encrypt messages under a Public Key Infrastructure (PKI) structured as *ASN.1* protocols. To maximize semantic coverage, Sandiff ignores *signatures* and compares only valid *ASN.1* elements.

C. Orchestrator

The *orchestrator* mechanism is responsible to share the resources of Sandiff among a variable number of competing comparison jobs to accelerate the analysis of large software projects. Consider the building process of AOSP. We noticed that, for regular builds, around 384K intermediate files are generated during compilation. In this scenario, running all routines of the official Android Test Suite, known as *Vendor Test Suite* (VTS), can represent a time consuming process that impacts productivity of mobile developers. To mitigate that, the *orchestrator* uses the well-known concept of *workers* and *jobs* that are managed by a priority queue. A *worker* is a thread that executes both recognition and comparison tasks over a pair of files, consuming the top-ranked files in the queue. To accelerate the analysis of large projects, Sandiff adopts the notion of a *fail greedy* sorting metric, i.e., routines with higher probability of failing are prioritized. The definition of *failing priority* is context-sensitive, but usually tend to emphasize critical and time-consuming routines. After the processing of all files, the results are aggregated into a structured report with the following semantic sections: (i) addition, (ii) removal, (iii) syntactically equality, and (iv) semantic equality.

IV. Experiments

In order to verify the comparison performance of Sandiff, we made experiments between different *commercially-available* images of AOSP. The experiments consist on comparing the following image pairs:

TABLE III. OVERALL SUMMARY OF THE IMPACT OF USING SANDIFF IN REAL-WORLD *COMMERCIALLY-AVAILABLE* AOSP BUILDS.

Comparison	Add		Remove		Edit		Type Edit		Equal		Error		Ignored	
	Semantinc	Binary	Semantic	Binary	Semantic	Binary	Semantic	Binary	Semantic	Binary	Semantic	Binary	Semantic	Binary
Experiment #1	0	0	0	0	**11**	12	0	0	2185	2185	**0**	19	0	0
Experiment #2	13	13	27	27	0	0	3	3	0	0	0	0	0	0
Experiment #3	23	23	18	18	**527**	606	0	0	**1929**	1805	**0**	45	0	0

* **Add** = file is present on the second input. **Remove** = file is present in the first input. **Edit** = file is present in both inputs, but the comparison returned differences. **Type Edit** = file is present in both inputs, but there were changes in its metadata (e.g., permissions). **Equal** = file is present in both inputs, and the comparison returns an *equal* status. **Error** = file is present in both inputs, but the comparison returns an *error* status. **Ignored** = file is present in both inputs, but is not semantically relevant, so it was ignored.

- **Experiment #1:** Comparing two revisions within same AOSP version: 8.1.0 r64 x 8.1.0 r65.

- **Experiment #2:** Comparing last revision of AOSP Oreo with initial release of AOSP Pie: 8.1.0 r65 x 9.0.0 r1.

- **Experiment #3:** Comparing last revision of AOSP Pie with its initial release: 9.0.0 r1 x 9.0.0 r45.

These pairs were compared using both semantic (Sandiff) and binary (checksum) comparison methods. To evaluate the robustness of each method, we analyzed the files contained in `system.img`, `userdata.img` and `vendor.img` images, which are mounted in the EXT2 file system under a UNIX system. Note that, differently from Sandiff, binary comparison is not capable of reading empty files and symbolic link targets. These files are listed as *errors*, as shown in Table III.

Based on the experiments of Table III, we can note that Sandiff was able to analyze large software projects like the AOSP. First, the semantic comparison was able to determine the file type and to compare not only the file contents, but it is metadata. In contrast, binary comparison was unable to compare symbolic link's targets and broken links failed. Second, the semantic comparison was able to discard irrelevant differences (e.g., the build time in build.prop) which are not differences in terms of functionality. Note that, during *experiment #2*, Sandiff is unable to perform a full analyses between these trees because there were structural changes. For instance, in AOSP Oreo, the `/bin` is a directory containing many files, while in AOSP Pie, the `/bin` is now a symbolic link to another path (that can be another image as well). As a result, Sandiff detects this case as a *Type Edit* and does not traverse `/bin` since it is only a directory in AOSP Oreo.

V. CONCLUSION

In this paper, we presented Sandiff, a semantic comparator tool that is designed to facilitate continuous testing of large software projects, specifically those related to AOSP. To the best of our knowledge, Sandiff is the first to allow correlation of test routines of the official Android Test Suite (VTS) with semantic modifications in intermediate files of AOSP building process. When used to skip time-consuming *test cases* or to mount a list of priority tests (*fail-fast*), Sandiff can lead to a higher productivity of mobile developers. We showed that semantic comparison is more robust to analyze large projects than binary comparison, since the former is unable to discard irrelevant modifications to the output or execution of the target software. As we refine the semantic comparators of Sandiff, more AOSP specific rules will apply, and consequently, more items can be classified as "Equal" in Sandiff's comparison reports. In the context of making Sandiff domain agnostic, another venue for future work is to explore machine learning techniques to detect how tests are related to different types of files and formats. We also plan to integrate Sandiff to the official Android Test Suite (VTS) to validate our intermediate results.

ACKNOWLEDGMENTS

We thank both Rafael Melo da Silva and Nick Diego Yamane Pinto for their valuable help during the development of the project. This work was supported by Sidia: Institute of Science and Technology.

REFERENCES

[1] Araxis Ltd. Araxis: Software. [Online]. Available: https://www.araxis.com/ [retrieved: October, 2019]

[2] Free Software Foundation, Inc. Diffutils. [Online]. Available: https://www.gnu.org/software/diffutils/ [retrieved: October, 2019]

[3] C. J. Madsen. Vbindiff - visual binary diff. [Online]. Available: https://www.cjmweb.net/ [retrieved: October, 2019]

[4] Y. Wang, D. J. DeWitt, and J. Cai, "X-diff: an effective change detection algorithm for xml documents," in Proceedings 19th International Conference on Data Engineering, March 2003, pp. 519–530.

[5] M. Pawlik and N. Augsten, "Efficient computation of the tree edit distance," ACM Transactions on Database Systems, vol. 40, 2015, pp. 3:1–3:40.

[6] D. Rachmawati, J. T. Tarigan, and A. B. C. Ginting, "A comparative study of message digest 5(MD5) and SHA256 algorithm," Journal of Physics: Conference Series, vol. 978, 2018, pp. 1–6.

[7] FreeType Project. Freetype. [Online]. Available: https://www.freetype.org/freetype2/ [retrieved: October, 2019]

[8] Apache Software Foundation. C xml parser. [Online]. Available: https://xerces.apache.org/xerces-c/ [retrieved: October, 2019]

Refinement Maps for Insulin Pump Control Software Safety Verification

Eman M. Al-qtiemat*, Sudarshan K. Srinivasan*, Zeyad A. Al-Odat*, Sana Shuja†
*Electrical and Computer Engineering, North Dakota State University,
Fargo, ND, USA
†Department of Electrical Engineering, COMSATS University,
Islamabad, Pakistan
Emails: *eman.alqtiemat@ndsu.edu, *sudarshan.srinivasan@ndsu.edu, *zeyad.alodat@ndsu.edu,
†SanaShuja@comsats.edu.pk

***Abstract*—Refinement-based verification is a formal verification technique that has shown promise to be applicable for verification of low-level real-time embedded object code. In refinement-based verification, both the implementation (the artifact to be verified) and the specification are modeled as transition systems, which essentially capture the states of the system and transitions between the states. A key step in the verification process is the construction of a refinement map, which is a function that maps implementation states onto specification states. Construction of refinement maps is most often done manually and requires key insights about how the implementation and specification behave. In this paper, we develop refinement maps for various safety properties concerning the software control operation of insulin pumps. We then identify possible generic templates for construction of refinement maps as a first step towards developing a process to construct refinement maps in an automated fashion.**

Keywords–Formal verification; safety-critical devices; Refinement maps; Refinement-based verification.

I. Introduction

One of the key issues in designing safety-critical embedded systems such as medical devices is software safety [1]. For example, infusion pumps (a medical device that delivers medication such as pain medication, insulin, cancer drugs etc., in controlled doses to patients intravenously) has 54 class 1 recalls related to software issued by the US Food and Drug Administration (FDA) [2]. Class 1 means that the use of the medical device can cause serious adverse health consequences or death.

Despite the fact that testing is the dominant verification technique currently used in commercial design cycles [3], testing can only show the presence of faults, but it never proves their absence [4]. Alternate verification processes should be applied to the software design in conjunction with testing to assure system correctness and reliability. Formal verification can address testing limitations by providing proofs of correctness for software safety. Intel [5], Microsoft [6] and [7], and Airbus [8] have successfully applied formal verification processes.

Refinement-based verification [9] is a formal verification technique that has been demonstrated to be effective for verification of software correctness at the object code level [10]. To apply refinement-based verification, software requirements should be expressed as a formal model. Previously, we have proposed a novel approach to synthesize formal specifications from natural language requirements [11], and in a later work, we have also addressed timing requirements and specifications [12].

Our verification approach is based on the theory of Well-Founded Equivalence Bisimulation (WEB) refinement [9]. In the context of WEB refinement, both the implementation and specification are treated as Transition Systems (TSs). If every behavior of the implementation is matched by a behavior of the specification and vice versa, then the implementation behaves correctly as prescribed by the specification. However, this is not easy to check in practice as the implementation TS and specification TS can look very different. The specification states obtained from the software requirements are marked with atomic propositions (predicates that are true or false in a given state). The implementation states are states of the microcontroller that the object code program modifies. As such, the microcontroller states includes registers, flags, and memory. The various possible values that these components can have during the execution of the object code program gives rise to the many millions of states of the implementation. To overcome this difference, WEB refinement uses the concept of a refinement map, which is a function that provided an implementation state, gives the corresponding specification state. Historically, one of the reasons that refinement-based verification is much less explored than other formal verification paradigms such as model checking is that the construction of refinement maps often requires deep understanding and intuitions about the specification and implementation [13]. However, once a refinement map is constructed, the benefit is that refinement-based verification is a very scalable approach for dealing with low-level artifacts such as real-time object code verification. This paper studies refinement maps corresponding to formal specifications related to infusion pump safety and proposes possible generic refinement map templates, which is the first step toward automating the construction of refinement maps.

The remainder of this paper is organized as follows. Section II summarizes background information. Section III details related work. Section IV describes the refinement maps and refinement map templates. Conclusions and direction for future work are noted in Section V.

II. Background

This section explores the definition of transition systems, the definition of refinement-based verification, and the synthesis of formal specifications as key terms related to our work.

A. Transition Systems

As stated earlier, transition systems (TSs) are used to model both specification and implementation in refinement-based verification. TSs are defined below.

Definition 1: A TS $M = \langle S, R, L \rangle$ is a three tuple in which S denotes the set of states, $R \subseteq SXS$ is the transition relation that provides the transition between states, and L is a labeling function that describes what is visible at each state.

States are marked with Atomic Propositions (APs), which are predicates that are true or false in each state. The labeling function maps states to the APs that are true in every state. An example TS is shown in Figure 1. Here S = {S1, S2, S3, S4}, R = {(S1, S2), (S2, S4), (S4, S3), (S3, S4), (S3, S2), (S1, S3)} and, $L(S2)$ represents the atomic propositions that are true for the S2 state.

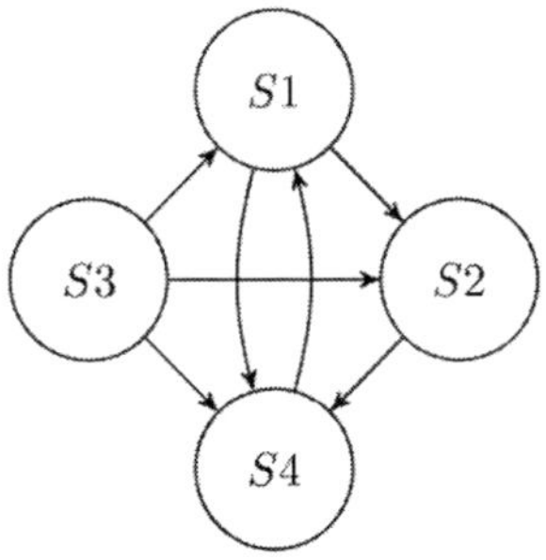

Figure 1. An example of a transition system (TS).

B. Refinement-Based Verification

Our verification process is based on the theory of Well-Founded Equivalence Bisimulation refinement. A detailed description of this theory can be found in [9]. Here, we give a very high-level overview of the key concepts. As stated earlier, WEB refinement provides a notion of correctness that can be used to check an implementation TS against a specification TS. One of the key features is that WEB refinement accounts for stuttering, which is the phenomenon where multiple but finite transitions of the implementation can match a single transition of the specification. This is a very key feature because the control code implements many functions and only some of these functions maybe relevant to the safety property being verified. Therefore, the code maybe doing a number of things that do not relate to the property and will therefore be stuttering a lot w.r.t. the specification. Another key feature of WEB refinement is refinement maps, which is the focus of this work. Refinement maps are functions that map implementation states to specification states. There is a lot of flexibility in how refinement maps can be defined. This allows for low-level implementations to be verified against high-level specifications.

Definition 2: (WEB Refinement): Let $M = \langle S, R, L \rangle$, $M' = \langle S', R', L' \rangle$, and r: S $\rightarrow$ S'. M is a WEB refinement of M' with respect to refinement map r, written $M \approx r\ M'$, if there exists a relation, B, such that $\langle$ $\forall$ s $\in$ S :: sB(r.s)$\rangle$ and B is a WEB on the TS $\langle$ S $\uplus$ S', R $\uplus$ R', L $\rangle$, where L.s = L'(s) for s and S' state and L.s = L'(r.s) otherwise.

C. Synthesis of Formal Specifications

Our approach for development and study of refinement maps is based on the formal TS specifications. We have developed a previous approach to transform functional requirements into formal specifications [11]. Since this work is closely tied to the prior work, we briefly review it here. The transformation procedure is as follows: The first step of computing the TSs is to extract the APs from the requirements. We have developed three Atomic Proposition Extraction Rules (APERs) that work on the parse tree of the requirement obtained from an English language parser called Enju. A high-level procedure for specification transition system synthesis has been proposed to compute the states and transitions using the resulting list of APs under expert user supervision. Figure 2 summarizes the main steps of the synthesizing procedure.

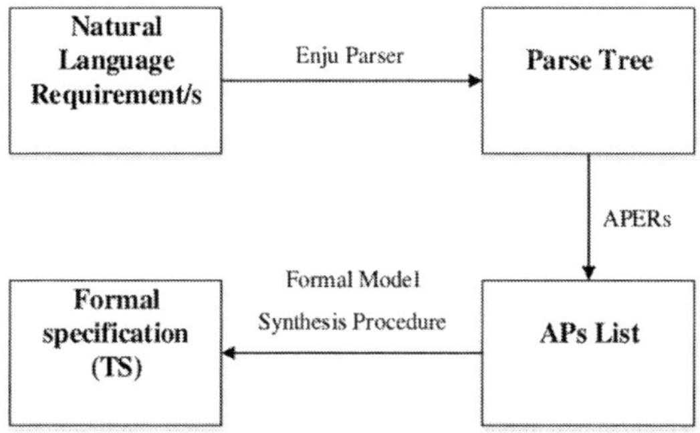

Figure 2. Formal Model synthesis procedure for Functional Requirements.

III. Related Work

This section summarizes a few works on applying refinement processes to get more concrete specifications and refinement-based verification. None of these works are applied to insulin pump formal specifications as our work. To the best of our knowledge, these are the most related state of art in this area of study.

Klein *et al.* [14] introduced a new technique called State Transition Diagrams (STD). It is a graphical specification technique that provides refinement rules, each rule defines an implementation relation on STD specification. The proposed approach was applied to the feature interaction problem. The refinement relation was utilized to add a feature or to define the notion of conflicting features.

Rabiah *et al.* [15] developed a reliable autonomous robot system by addressing A* path planning algorithm reliability issue. A refinement process was used to capture more concrete specifications by transforming High-Level specification into equivalent executable program. Traditional mathematical concepts were used to capture formal descriptions.Then, Z specification language was employed to transform mathematical description to Z schemas to get formal specifications. Z formal refinement theory was used to obtain the implementation specification.

Spichkova [16] proposed a refinement-based verification scheme for interactive real time systems. The proposed work solves the mistakes that rise from the specification problems by integrating the formal specifications with the verification system. The proposed scheme translates the specifications to a higher-order logic, and then uses the theorem prover (Isabelle) to prove the specifications. Using the refinement-based verification, this scheme validates the refinement relations between two different systems. The proposed design was tested and verified using a case study of electronic data transmission gateway.

A new approach that focuses on the refinement verification using state flow charts has been presented by Miyazawa *et al.* [17]. They proposed a refinement strategy that supports the sequential *C* implementations of the state flow charts. The proposed design benefited from the architectural features of model to allow a higher level of automation by retrieving the data relation in a calculation style and rendering the data into an automated system. The proposed design was tested and verified using Matlab Simulink SDK. Through the provided case study, the scheme was able to be scaled to different state charts problems.

Cimatti *et al.* proposed a contract-refinement scheme for embedded systems [18]. The contract-refinement provides interactive composition reasoning, step-wise refinement, and principled reuse refinements for components for the already designed or independently designed components. The proposed design addresses the problem of architectural decomposition of embedded systems based on the principles of temporal logic to generate a set of proof obligations. The testing and verification of the Wheel Braking System (WBS) case study show that the proposed design can detect the problems in the architectural design of the WBS.

Bibighaus [19] employed the Doubly Labeled Transition Systems (DLTS) to reason about possibilities security properties and refinement. This work was compared with three different security frameworks when applied to large class systems. The refinement framework in this work preserves and guarantees the liveness of the model by verifying the timing parameter of the model. The analysis results show that the proposed design preserves the security properties to a series of availability requirements.

IV. Refinement Maps and Refinement Map Templates

Figures 3-9 show the formal TS specification for 8 insulin pump safety requirements and the refinement map we have developed corresponding to each specification TS. The formal TS specifications were developed as part of our previous work in this area [11] [12]. As can be seen from the figures, each TS consists of a set of states and the transitions between the states. Also, each state is marked with the atomic propositions that are true in the state.

Our strategy for constructing the refinement maps is as follows. A specification state can be constructed from an implementation state by determining the APs that are true in the implementation state. If a specification has n APs, then we construct one predicate function for each AP. The predicate functions take the implementation state as input and output a predicate value that indicates if the AP is true in that state or not. Thus, the collection of such predicate functions is the refinement map.

We next discuss the refinement map for the specification in Figure 3. The safety specification from [20] is as follows: "The pump shall suspend all active basal delivery and stop any active bolus during a pump prime or refill. It shall prohibit any insulin administration during the priming process and resume the suspended basal delivery, either a basal profile or a temporary basal, after the prime or refill is successfully completed." The APs corresponding to this safety requirement are (1) BO: active bolus delivery; (2) BA: active basal delivery; (3) P: priming process; and (4) R: refill process. The refinement map however has to account for what is happening in the implementation code and relate that to the atomic propositions.

The predicate function for BO uses several variables from the code including NB: Normal Bolus and EB: Extended Bolus as there are more than one type of Bolus dose supported by the system. So the AP BO should be true if there is a NB or an EB. NB is only a flag that indicates that a normal bolus should be in progress. The actual bolus itself will continue to occur as long as a counter that keeps track of the bolus has not reached its maximum value. Therefore, for example for a normal bolus, we use a conjunction of NB and the condition that the NB counter (NB_c) is less than its possible maximum value (NB_m). We use a similar strategy for the extended bolus as well. This refinement map template works for all processes similar to a Bolus dosage delivery, such as basal dosage delivery, priming process, and refill process. Therefore, we term this refinement map template as "process template." For the basal dosage (BA AP) a number of basal profiles (BPs) are possible that accounts for BP_1 thru BP_n. TB stands for temporary basal. As can be noted from Figures 4-9, the process template accounts for a large number of predicate functions corresponding to APs.

The second refinement map template is a simple one called the "projection template," which is used when the AP in the specification TS corresponds directly to a variable in the code. An example of the projection template can be found in Figure 4, where the User Reminder (UR) AP is mapped directly from a flag variable in the code that corresponds to the user reminder. A variation of this template is a boolean expression of Boolean variables in the code. An example of such an AP is the UIP AP in Figure 8.

The third refinement map template is called the "value change template," which is used when the AP is true only when a value has changed. An example use of this template can be found in Figure 4 for the CDTC AP. CDTC corresponds to the change in drug type and concentration and is true when the drug type or concentration is changed. For the drug type change, DT is the variable that corresponds to the drug type. The question here is how to track that a value has changed. The idea is to use history variables. HDT is a history variable that corresponds to the history of the drug type, i.e., the value of the drug type in the previous cycle. If HDT is not equal to DT in a code state, then we know the drug type has changed. The inequality of HDT and DT is used to construct the predicate function. For all the safety requirements analyzed, these three refinement map templates cover all the APs. Table 1 gives the expansions for all the abbreviations used in Figures 3-9, so that the corresponding refinement maps can be comprehended by the reader.

V. Conclusion and Future Work

In this paper, we have developed refinement maps corresponding to the specification TSs of several infusion pump safety requirements. This is a first step in automating the construction of refinement maps. Our eventual goal is to develop a process for the construction of refinement maps. The refinement maps from this paper will be used as benchmarks to study and develop generic refinement map templates. Heuristics will be developed based on the output of the Enju parser to select a refinement map template for each atomic proposition. The development and testing of this process is part of future work.

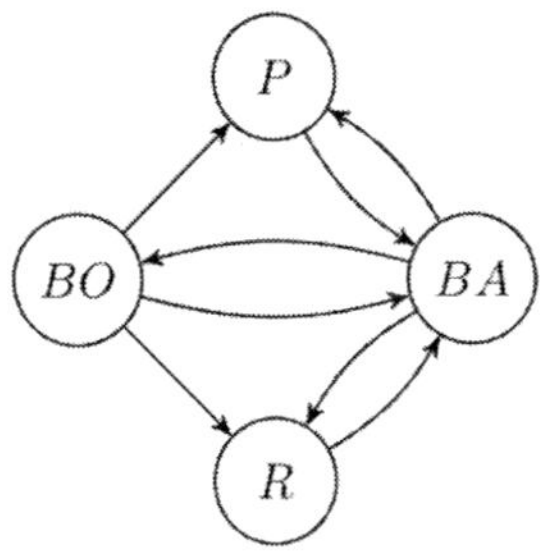

- **BO** = [NB $\wedge$ $(NB_c < NB_m)$] $\vee$ [EB $\wedge$ $(EB_c < EB_m)$]
- **P** = P $\wedge$ $(P_c < P_m)$
- **R** = R $\wedge$ $(R_c < R_m)$
- **BA** = $[BP_1 \wedge (BP_{1c} < BP_{1m})] \vee [BP_2 \wedge (BP_{2c} < BP_{2m})] \vee \ldots \vee [BP_n \wedge (BP_{nc} < BP_{nm})]$ $\vee$ [TB $\wedge$ $(TB_c < TB_m)$]

Figure 3. A formal presentation of requirement 1.1.1 from [20] and the suggested refinement maps.

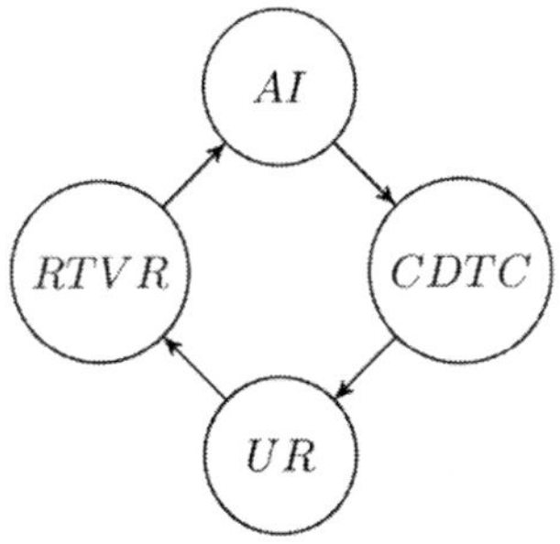

- **AI** = $[BP_1 \wedge (BP_{1c} < BP_{1m})] \vee [BP_2 \wedge (BP_{2c} < BP_{2m})] \vee \ldots \vee [BP_n \wedge (BP_{nc} < BP_{nm})]$ $\vee$ [TB $\wedge$ $(TB_c < TB_m)$] $\vee$ [NB $\wedge$ $(NB_c < NB_m)$] $\vee$ [EB $\wedge$ $(EB_c < EB_m)$]
- **CDTC** = (DT $\neq$ HDT) $\wedge$ $(CDTC_c < CDTC_m)$
- **UR** = FLAG
- **RTVR** = (CRV $\neq$ HRV) $\wedge$ $(RTVR_c < RTVR_m)$

Figure 4. A formal presentation of requirement 1.1.3 from [20] and the suggested refinement maps.

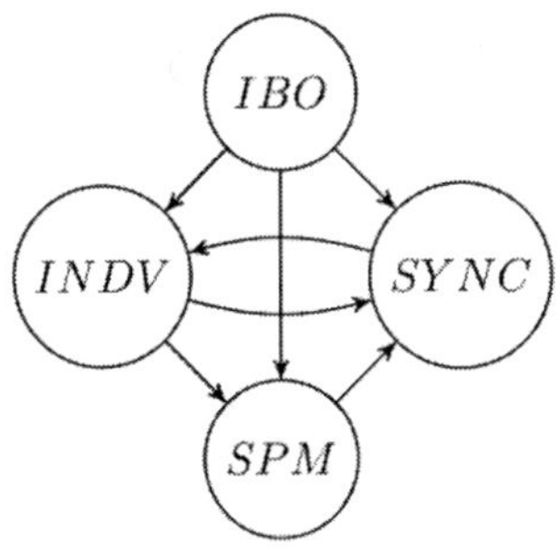

- **IBO** = [NB $\wedge$ $(NB_c < NB_m)$] $\vee$ [EB $\wedge$ $(EB_c < EB_m)$]
- **INDV** = $[BP_1 \wedge (BP_{1c} < BP_{1m})] \vee [BP_2 \wedge (BP_{2c} < BP_{2m})] \vee \ldots \vee [BP_n \wedge (BP_{nc} < BP_{nm})]$ $\vee$ [TB $\wedge$ $(TB_c < TB_m)$] $\vee$ [NB $\wedge$ $(NB_c < NB_m)$] $\vee$ [EB $\wedge$ $(EB_c < EB_m)$]
- **SMP** = [P $\wedge$ $(P_c < P_m)$] $\vee$ [R $\wedge$ $(R_c < R_m)$]
- **SYNC** = INCAL $\wedge$ $(INCAL_c < INCAL_m)$

Figure 5. A formal presentation of requirement 1.8.2 and 1.8.5 from [20] and the suggested refinement maps.

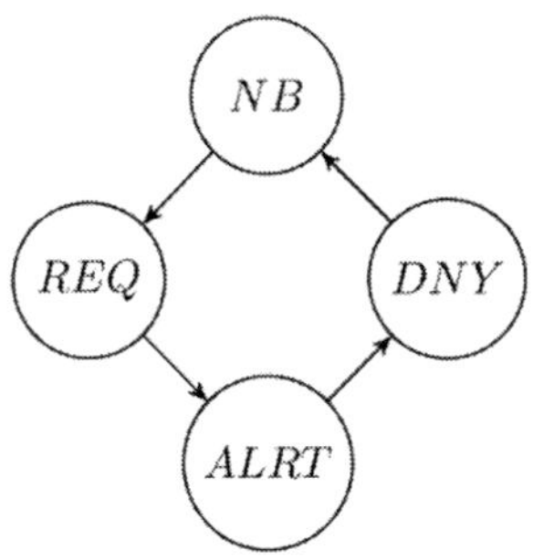

- **NB** = NB $\wedge$ $(NB_c < NB_m)$
- **REQ** = REQ-FLAG
- **ALRT** = ALRT-FLAG
- **DNY** = CALL-FUNCT

Figure 6. A formal presentation of requirement 1.3.5 from [20] and the suggested refinement maps.

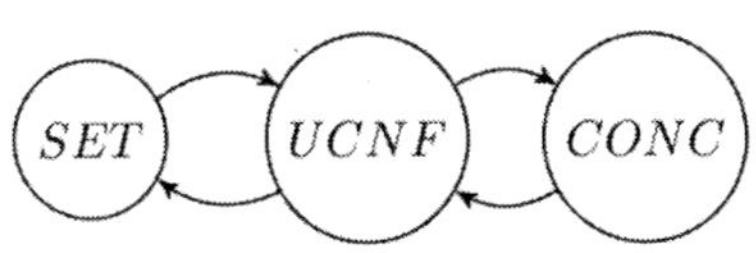

- **SET** = CLRS $\vee$ [CHNS $\wedge$ $(CHNS_c < CHNS_m)$] $\vee$ RESS
- **UCNF** = FLAG
- **CONC** = [SETT $\wedge$ $(SETT_c < SETT_m)$] $\vee$ [CHNC $\wedge$ $(CHNC_c < CHNC_m)$]

Figure 7. A formal presentation of requirement 2.2.2 and 2.2.3 from [20] and the suggested refinement maps.

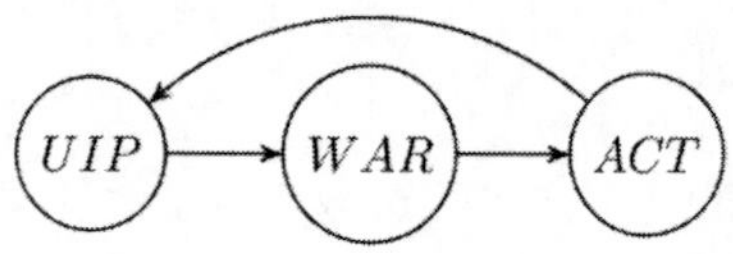

- **UIP** = BG $\vee$ TBG $\vee$ INCR $\vee$ CORF
- **WAR** = FLAG
- **ACT** = CNFI $\vee$ [CHNI $\wedge$ $(CHNI_c < CHNI_m)$]

Figure 8. A formal presentation of requirement 3.2.5 from [20] followed by the suggested refinement maps.

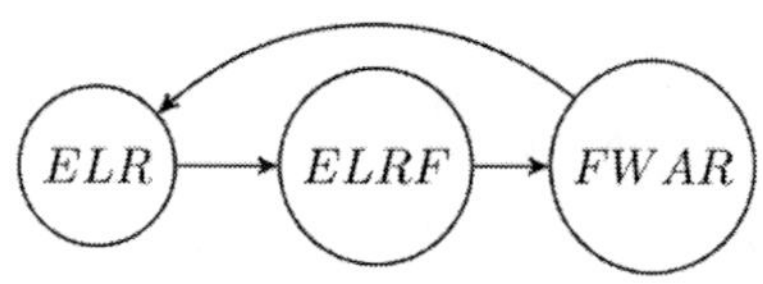

- **ELR** = [EL $\wedge$ $(EL_c < EL_m)$] $\vee$ [LR $\wedge$ $(LR_c < LR_m)$]
- **ELRF** = ELF $\vee$ LRF
- **FWAR** = FLAG

Figure 9. A formal presentation of requirement 3.2.7 from [20] followed by the suggested refinement maps.

TABLE I. LIST OF ABBREVIATIONS

Abbreviation	Meaning
AI	Active Infusion
CDTC	Change Drug Type and Concentration
DT	Data Type
HDT	Historical Data Type
UR	User Reminder
RTVR	Reservoir Time and Volume Recomputed
CRV	Current Reservoir Volume
HRV	Historical Reservoir Volume
REQ-FLAG	Request Flag
CALL-FUNCT	Call-Function for Calculation
INCAL	Insulin Calculations
CLRS	Clear Settings
CHNS	Change Settings
RESS	Reset Settings
BG	Blood Glucose
TBG	Targeted Blood Glucose
INCR	Insulin to Carbohydrate ratio
CORF	Correction Factor
CNFI	Confirm Input
CHNI	Change Input
EL	Event Logging
LR	Log Retrieving
ELRF	Event Logging or Logging Retrieving Failure
ELF	Event Logging Failure
LRF	Logging Retrieving Failure

ACKNOWLEDGMENT

This publication was funded by a grant from the United States Government and the generous support of the American people through the United States Department of State and the United States Agency for International Development (USAID) under the Pakistan - U.S. Science & Technology Cooperation Program. The contents do not necessarily reflect the views of the United States Government.

REFERENCES

[1] B. Fei, W. S. Ng, S. Chauhan, and C. K. Kwoh, "The safety issues of medical robotics," Reliability Engineering & System Safety, vol. 73, no. 2, 2001, pp. 183–192.

[2] FDA, "List of Device Recalls, U.S. Food and Drug Administration (FDA)," 2018, last accessed: 2019-10-11. [Online]. Available: https://www.accessdata.fda.gov/scripts/cdrh/cfdocs/cfRES/res.cfm

[3] S. Quadri and S. U. Farooq, "Software testing-goals, principles, and limitations," International Journal of Computer Applications, vol. 6, no. 9, 2010, pp. 7–10.

[4] E. Miller and W. E. Howden, Tutorial, software testing & validation techniques. IEEE Computer Society Press, 1981.

[5] R. Kaivola et al., "Replacing testing with formal verification in intel coretm i7 processor execution engine validation," in Computer Aided Verification, 21st International Conference, CAV, Grenoble, France, June 26 - July 2, 2009. Proceedings, pp. 414–429. [Online]. Available: https://doi.org/10.1007/978-3-642-02658-4_32

[6] T. Ball, B. Cook, V. Levin, and S. K. Rajamani, "SLAM and static driver verifier: Technology transfer of formal methods inside microsoft," in Integrated Formal Methods, 4th International Conference, IFM, Canterbury, UK, April 4-7, 2004, Proceedings, pp. 1–20. [Online]. Available: https://doi.org/10.1007/978-3-540-24756-2_1

[7] K. Bhargavan et al., "Formal verification of smart contracts: Short paper," in Proceedings of the 2016 ACM Workshop on Programming Languages and Analysis for Security. ACM, 2016, pp. 91–96.

[8] D. Delmas, E. Goubault, S. Putot, J. Souyris, K. Tekkal, and F. Védrine, "Towards an industrial use of fluctuat on safety-critical avionics software," in International Workshop on Formal Methods for Industrial Critical Systems. Springer, 2009, pp. 53–69.

[9] P. Manolios, "Mechanical verification of reactive systems," PhD thesis, University of Texas at Austin, August 2001, last accessed: 2019-10-04. [Online]. Available: http://www.ccs.neu.edu/home/pete/research/phd-dissertation.html

[10] M. A. L. Dubasi, S. K. Srinivasan, and V. Wijayasekara, "Timed refinement for verification of real-time object code programs," in Working Conference on Verified Software: Theories, Tools, and Experiments. Springer, 2014, pp. 252–269.

[11] E. M. Al-qtiemat, S. K. Srinivasan, M. A. L. Dubasi, and S. Shuja, "A methodology for synthesizing formal specification models from requirements for refinement-based object code verification," in The Third International Conference on Cyber-Technologies and Cyber-Systems. IARIA, 2018, pp. 94–101.

[12] E. M. Al-Qtiemat, S. K. Srinivasan, Z. A. Al-Odat, and S. Shuja, "Synthesis of Formal Specifications From Requirements for Refinement-based Real Time Object Code Verification," International Journal on Advances in Internet Technology, vol. 12, Aug 2019, pp. 95–107.

[13] M. Abadi and L. Lamport, "The existence of refinement mappings," Theoretical Computer Science, vol. 82, no. 2, 1991, pp. 253–284.

[14] C. Klein, C. Prehofer, and B. Rumpe, "Feature specification and refinement with state transition diagrams," arXiv preprint arXiv:1409.7232, 2014.

[15] E. Rabiah and B. Belkhouche, "Formal specification, refinement, and implementation of path planning," in 12th International Conference on Innovations in Information Technology (IIT). IEEE, 2016, pp. 1–6.

[16] M. Spichkova, "Refinement-based verification of interactive real-time systems," Electronic Notes in Theoretical Computer Science, vol. 214, 2008, pp. 131–157.

[17] A. Miyazawa and A. Cavalcanti, "Refinement-based verification of sequential implementations of stateflow charts," arXiv preprint arXiv:1106.4094, 2011.

[18] A. Cimatti and S. Tonetta, "Contracts-refinement proof system for component-based embedded systems," Science of computer programming, vol. 97, 2015, pp. 333–348.

[19] D. L. Bibighaus, "Applying doubly labeled transition systems to the refinement paradox," Naval Postgraduate School Monterey CA, Tech. Rep., 2005.

[20] Y. Zhang, R. Jetley, P. L. Jones, and A. Ray, "Generic safety requirements for developing safe insulin pump software," Journal of diabetes science and technology, vol. 5, no. 6, 2011, pp. 1403–1419.

**International Academy, Research,
and Industry Association (IARIA)**
412 Derby Way
Wilmington, DE 19810

ISBN 978-1-7138-0061-3

CURRAN ASSOCIATES INC.
proceedings.com

First International Conference on AI-based Systems and Services (AISyS 2024)

Held at SoftNet 2024

Venice, Italy
29 September - 3 October 2024